GoatMan

GoatMan

How I Took a Holiday from Being Human

Thomas Thwaites

PRINCETON ARCHITECTURAL PRESS · NEW YORK

It is better to be a human
being dissatisfied than
a pig satisfied; better
to be Socrates dissatisfied
than a fool satisfied.
And if the fool, or the pig,
is of a different opinion,
it is because they
only know their own side
of the question.

—John Stuart Mill, *Utilitarianism* (1863)

Dedicated to my parents,
Lyndsay Thwaites and Philip Thwaites

Contents

INTRODUCTION

Waterloo, London

(sunny but cold)

This great ball of Earth revolves, and once again the morning commute is in full flow. *Trip trap trip trap*, along the concourse, *clip clop clip clop*, up the steps, onto the bridge, over the Thames, and into the centre of London to work. Men and women stream past, all striding determinedly in the same direction. Suits and ties for the guys who work in finance, suit jacket and jeans for the Soho creative chaps, and jeans and T-shirt for the blokes in IT or those who otherwise don't care to project a can-do, I'm-your-guy, power-man-chap persona. I'm less *au fait* with the uniform typologies for the ladies, but I expect there is an equivalent, perhaps more nuanced set of clothing signifiers operating that fails to register, in my conscious mind at least (though a friend who once worked in a Louis Vuitton shop told me they were trained to judge a woman walking into the shop by her hair rather than her clothes. Immaculately coiffured with threadbare clothes = eccentric aristocrat. Just threadbare clothes = bag lady).

Anyway, why am *I* not tramping along myself, in my jeans and T-shirt (or possibly it'd be suit jacket and jeans for me), making my merry way to the office? Because I'm dogsitting my nieces' dog for a week. Because I'm available to do it. Because I don't have a (real) job. So I have no office to go to. My girlfriend does have a real job, so she has continued *clip clop* up the steps to cross the bridge to work, but I have peeled off and am sitting outside a chain coffee outlet, dog at my feet, watching as the rest of the world streams by.

This scene rather sums up my present state of being. Other adults striding past, moving forwards with purpose, progressing, on their way to their jobs, their careers, and the rest of their adult lives, while I sit and have a coffee, my major task of the day being to stop Noggin (the dog) from eating anything too disgusting off the pavement. I'm now thirty-three years old, and my lack of a (real) job is starting to become a bit of a worry because, well, because "The Future." Sure, my work as a freelance designer is keeping me fed and watered *now*, but in not too long I might need to provide for some future family. I'm meant to be a grown-up human man, but I (effectively) live with my dad (I have yet to get a toenail onto London's telescoping property ladder). I was turned down from opening a bank account yesterday (and again in a letter this morning because, no, it wasn't a mistake the first time), and I have yet to hear back from the recruitment person I sent my CV to two weeks ago.

OK, OK, OK—I know that compared to many I'm essentially a rich kid with an extensive safety net (after all, I can always live with my dad forever, right?), my girlfriend having pointed this out *at length* during our argument last night. However, being described as a trustafarian does not actually help with my present malaise. Because although a safety net is great to bounce around on for a while, surely there's got to be some steady climbing done, too, if one's to reach some sort of stable perch in the great circus tent of life. All the climbing I've done has somehow ended up being more of a clamber sideways, rather than purposeful upwards motion. By now I should be far higher if I'm ever to become the comfortable and secure middle-aged man of aspiration. I mean, I should have at least flown the coop, right? and have some sort of steady income. I mean, I'm thirty-three years old! Instead…nothing. And nothing will come of nothing. My sense of self-esteem is sunk.

But come on, Thomas, have you not had some success? A project you did (the Toaster Project) was recently acquired by the Victoria and Albert Museum for its permanent collection—for the nation, for posterity for Christ's sake. That's a plus! And you had a book about the Toaster

Project published and got some nice feedback from people all over the world. Another plus! You presented that four-part TV series based on the Toaster Project (plus 1 again!). But...the TV series was hideously embarrassing and (thank God) has only ever been broadcast in Vietnam, Australia, and Korea (South, I think). Minus. The book must have been a fluke, an aberration, and so you're a one-hit wonder (minus 5). And anyway, the Toaster Project was four years ago! What about now? You have peaked and are in decline. While you've been dining out on toast, your peers have been getting PhDs, getting commissions, getting careers, *moving on up*. Your oldest friend is now a (real) doctor! The other night he had to reach *inside* a man's chest cavity to pump his heart with his *bare hands* in a heroic attempt to save the man's life. Unfortunately he died, but still. What are *you* doing, Thomas? Having a coffee. Getting old (minus 1) and going grey (minus 10) and not not saving anyone's life at all. It's like I was near the front of the pack but took my foot off the accelerator, pulled into the lay-by to smell some shrubs, and now look around: all of a sudden everyone I know is really *involved,* doing important things, but way off in the distance, and now my car won't start. I'm stuck. Stuck in a big, dark hole.

Oh, woe is bloody you, Thomas. These concerns, I realise, are self-absorbed and, on the spectrum of things people have to worry about, absolutely minor. Thank God they don't involve worrying about where my next meal is going to come from. But in any case, these are my worries, and right now they're back to worry *me*.

Do *all* people in the world have their own personal constellations of worries that ebb and flow, drifting away for a while only to return later with a vengeance? My nephew is 4¾ years old, and he's worried about dying—not just that he will die, but that death exists at all. That one day Mum, Dad, he, and everyone will, inevitably, die (a shocking fact if you've only just found out). All right, the Queen: What does she worry about? Born into a life of the utmost privilege and prestige. But what makes her feel that sense of unease? The burden of tradition? Her heir's prospects?

Yes, even the Queen has worries. To be human is to worry.

But look at Noggin. I would conjecture that while he has likes (street food), dislikes (being left alone), and even perhaps *desires* about the immediate future (I wish I could go over there and eat that piece of street food), I just don't think Noggin worries. Noggin and the Queen are the same in all other major respects: eating, sleeping, defecating, communicating, using tools (well, not Noggin himself—he's as thick as two planks—but a dingo canine cousin of his was observed dragging a table around to use as a stepladder). However, only the Queen worries.

Her Majesty the Queen: Worried   Noggin: Worry free

I base this conclusion on the fact that to be worried about some *thing*, you have to imagine that *thing* happening or not happening. This means you have to be able to imagine the future to worry about it. At the moment I seem to be doing a lot of imagining the future, and presently I'm finding it difficult to imagine a viable one for myself. And it's not only my own perceived lack of prospects—the future of the world seems pretty worrying at present. Read the news and it's clear we're all heading up shit creek without a paddle. The gap between rich and poor is set to widen to a chasm (please let me end up on the rich side), we're in the midst of a sixth great extinction (caused by you and me, et al.), ecosystems are being stretched to breaking point, and those terrorist folk—they're gruesome thugs, but more people are joining them! And climate change is going to exacerbate all these problems one way or another, so we're all doomed. Doomed. Yes, there's plenty to worry about.

Wouldn't it be nice to just switch off that particularly human ability for a couple of weeks? To live totally in the moment, with no worries about what you've done, what you're doing, or what you should do? Wouldn't it be nice to escape the constraints and expectations of not just your society, your culture, your personal history, but your very biology? To escape the inevitable worries of personhood? To step away from the complexities of the world and have a lovely holiday, not just to somewhere warm, away from your job (if you have one), away from your daily life, but away from your very self itself? To have a holiday from *being human*? Escaping the complexities of the human world and living life with just the bare necessities. Living without the trappings of civilisation and without all the complications either. Treading lightly on the Earth; causing no bloody suffering, contentedly deriving your sustenance from the green plants growing all around. Absorbed in your immediate surroundings, eating a bit of grass, sleeping on the ground, and that's it? Galloping across the landscape: free! Wouldn't it be nice to be an animal just for a bit?

* * *

Oh, crikey. After a rush of anticipation at seeing the subject line in the email, scanning it for the well-known phrases of rejection like "level of submissions was very high" or "after careful consideration," luxuriating in the feeling of success for about a minute, I have a look back at the application I submitted some weeks earlier as a way out of my malaise. What did I say I'd do again? Oh. Oh, crikey.

What I said I'd do is make an exoskeleton that would undo five million years of human evolution and adapt my bipedal anatomy to that of a quadruped. And also develop an artificial prosthetic stomach that would enable me to eat and digest grass. And that I would also adapt my sight and hearing and retrain my senses. And use transcranial magnetic stimulation to switch off the forward planning and language centres of

The Wellcome Trust
Private and Confidential

Dear Mr. Thwaites,

Arts Awards

Thank you for your application to the Arts Awards
programme. I am delighted to confirm that your
application for funding of the project "I want to be an
elephant." was successful. The Committee thought that
this was a wonderfully engaging idea from an experimental
designer with a good track record. The Committee were
confident that the Principal Applicant would produce
something high quality and interesting. Members noted
that the timescales looked very tight and advised them
to rethink their timetable.

If, for any reason, you are unable to accept the award,
please get in touch with me as soon as possible.

Best wishes,

Jenny Paton
Arts Adviser
Public Engagement
Medical Humanities and Engagement Grants
Wellcome Trust

my brain so as to experience life from the perspective of an elephant. And then, while being an elephant in my elephant exoskeleton, cross the Alps.

Oh, dear, I've been an idiot and promised way too much, and now they've called my bluff (minus 1). I don't have the strength to push this project along (minus 1). It's ridiculous and meaningless and definitely not a serious design project (minus 1). It's a waste of money that could otherwise be used to fund a cure for cancer (minus 1). I'll never be able to manage it before winter closes in over the Alps and I should've just bloody well stuck to making kitchen appliances.

* * *

It would be good if it worked, though...

Soul

Copenhagen, Denmark
(freezing)

Yep, definitely in Copenhagen. As I wait to cross the road, a muscular, Lycra-clad Dane scoots past on cross-country skis with wheels attached (the wheels alleviate the lack of snow).

I've been invited to Denmark to teach a design "master class" (their words), and I've arranged my travel via Copenhagen, as I'm going to meet someone who I hope could help me with my elephant project. I'm looking for a place called Ballonparken: a site in central Copenhagen with one hundred small wooden huts, built in the Second World War to house antiaircraft balloons. Now the huts are occupied by a community living as "an independent self-governing institution," serving as homes for individuals wishing to live counter to the prevailing culture. One of those individuals is a shaman, and it is she whom I seek.

My perspective on life has shifted since the melancholy of the introduction. My generalised angst about the world has passed, the argument with my girlfriend is water under the bridge, and my self-indulgent funk has cleared. The fact that I'm referring to an introduction means I sent that writing to Princeton Architectural Press and they've indicated they'll make a book of it, if I can get it together to finish this bloody thing. And if I do, well, "Hullo there, gentle reader!"

And maybe it's just because my phone broke and I can't check the news every five minutes, but no longer does the world seemed doomed, either. Sure, there's a lot wrong out there, but things are going in the right direction. The gap may be widening, but the poor are still getting less poor; global population will peak in a few years and then decline, and technology will develop so we can all live comfortable and fruitful lives without sending the climate too far out of kilter. Hooray! (And terrorists? Terrorists who? They're just the current crop of terminally misguided bananas, and every generation has its own bunch.)

In short, the world and I are on the up! But while *I'm feeling fine*, the grand project to become an elephant has quietly ground to a halt. Don't tell the Wellcome Trust, but I've pretty much been avoiding it, finding myself pleasantly engaged in other things (like this, ahem, *master* class). You see, a rather fundamental problem has developed with the very premise of this I-want-to-be-an-elephant project, and that is I no longer want to be an elephant.

* * *

I'd decided to become an *elephant* mainly for practical reasons. Somehow, when I was writing my proposal to the Wellcome Trust, the design constraints inherent in becoming an elephant, as opposed to some other nonhuman animal that fitted my vision of roaming free in the landscape, seemed less insurmountable.

This was based on the following assumptions: first, the build envelope of an elephant is rather large, with ample room to contain me inside, as well as negating any need for fiddly microengineering. Second, being big, elephants are slow and lumbering, right? Hence, if my exoskeleton turned out to be slow and lumbering, as I rather suspected it would, no matter. Third and most crucial, my concern was with neck length.

I considered neck length to be so important because while it was easy to imagine extending my arms to become a quadruped, I just couldn't imagine a way to extend my neck to match. And elephants are pretty unique in that they're grazing animals with a short neck relative to their legs.

A fundamental part of being an alive animal is not becoming food for another animal. So to avoid being eaten alive, a set of long and fast legs can be an advantage. But another fundamental part of being an alive animal is eating food yourself. If you're a herbivorous quadruped, then you eat grass and foliage. This has a low energy density, which means you need to eat a lot of it. In fact, your face needs to be in your food for about 60 percent of your waking life. And since your food is often at your feet, a neck long enough to allow you to get your face down to your food with a minimum of fuss is an advantage.

So to optimise the two advantageous characteristics of speediness and grazing efficiency, evolution has acted through the painful mechanism of animals being eaten alive or starving to death (or some grim combination of the two) to keep the necks of all herbivorous quadrupeds approximately as long as their legs.[1] All, that is, except the elephant. With elephants, evolution took a radically different course: grow the legs (hell, grow the whole frickin' animal if you like!) *and* keep the neck short? You bet: don't move your face to your food; move your food to your face! How? With your nose!

So our shared characteristic of having a (relatively) short neck was what had led me to the elephant.

However, I'd recently had the opportunity to go to South Africa (things were on the up, like I said), and so I'd, of course, gone on safari hoping to see elephants. And I did. But seeing them in the wild—and up frighteningly close—made me realise that most of the advantages I'd imagined elephants to have, with regard to becoming one, were indeed imagined. The "advantage" of a large build envelope evaporated when I saw just how huge elephants can be. To allow me to really feel what life would be like as an elephant, my exoskeleton would have to be at least the size of a large family car and powerful enough to enable me to push over a tree pretty casually. The only way this was going to happen would be if I added an engine, and then I'd pretty much have built a car with legs. That is a laudable and not unexplored goal, but it just isn't what I was after.

---

1   Of course, an animal with long legs but a short neck could get around this by kneeling down to eat, but there is a phrase, "sitting duck," and it doesn't just apply to ducks.

2   That is, random mutation, followed by natural selection.

Evolution: totally random! [2]

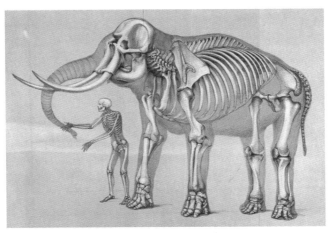

Elephants and us: short necks. Plate 6 from *A Comparative View of the Human and Animal Frame* (1860) by Benjamin Waterhouse Hawkins.

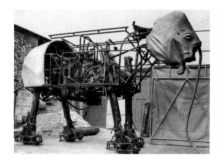

Mechanical elephants, surprisingly prevalent.

And while yes, elephants have that all-important short neck, they also have that all-important trunk. The more thought I gave to how I was actually going to make a working trunk, the more impossible the prospect seemed. Massachusetts Institute of Technology made a trunk, but firstly, I'm no Massachusetts Institute of Technology, and secondly, it was pneumatic. This would require dragging around a compressor, which would need an engine, and there you are—back to building a car with legs. Cars are supposed to offer freedom—the open road and all that—but it's freedom only within the system. I was after freedom from the system itself! So dragging a growling (or whining) engine around (and having to worry about filling up with petrol or recharging batteries) wasn't going to feel right. I wanted my animal exoskeleton to be powered by me alone.

Even if the physical problems could be overcome and somehow an exoskeleton could be built that made me *feel* as big and strong as an elephant, I came to realise there was another, deeper problem with elephants: they are, I think, almost too human.

A primary goal of the project was to escape the worry and existential pain of being a human, but I started to feel that psychologically it mightn't necessarily be all that rosy being an elephant, either.

For one thing, it's thought that elephants understand mortality. Just like humans, they'll tend another elephant that's dying. Two elephants have been seen struggling to keep another, who was terminally ill, on its feet; then, when it did lie down to die, they tried to feed it by putting grass in its mouth with their trunks. And when the sick elephant did finally pass away, they stood over its body for days. Families of elephants have been documented visiting the body of a recently deceased matriarch elephant, over the course of several days. It very much seems as if they mourn their dead. And when they do eventually leave fallen kin, they sometimes cover the body with leaves and branches. The behaviour patterns of a family of elephants can take years to return to normal after a violent death in the group, such as at the hands of poachers or as part of a cull, indicating they suffer from something like posttraumatic stress. Only a handful of species, including dolphins, chimps, and gorillas, have been seen to treat a corpse of one of their kind with reverence. But elephants are the only

other species besides ourselves (and the extinct Neanderthals) who have
a documented ritual reaction to the *bones* of their species. Elephants who
come across the sun-bleached bones and tusks of an elephant long dead
will examine them with their trunks in a markedly different way from
how they usually fling around interesting objects (including the bones of
nonelephants).

I came to realise that my internal mental idea of elephants was
heavily coloured by warm feelings from my childhood towards Dumbo.
The reality is elephants are complex, intelligent wild animals, frighteningly powerful and sometimes aggressive. They're perhaps aware of their
own mortality, they live in families (and we all know that families are an
unending source of stress and worry), and they are prone, it seems, to suffering sadness, depression, and personality disorders just as we are (hold
on—actually, that's pretty much all there in *Dumbo*). I'm already an animal prone to these, so trying to escape by becoming an elephant would be
akin to jumping from the existential frying pan into another frying pan.
So I returned from South Africa with a somewhat disturbed view of elephants and somewhat disturbed by my newfound desire not to become
one. So I went to the pub. And, of course, after a couple of pints, a friend
made an excellent suggestion: I should seek guidance from an acquain-
tance of hers who's a shaman who lives in Scandinavia. After all, a shaman is a kind of expert on human-animal relations. And so, when I found
myself visiting Denmark to teach a master class, I went via Copenhagen.

＊　＊　＊

I find the entrance to the Ballonparken. Rows of little wooden cabins,
painted iron oxide red with white window frames, sit on either side of
a muddy track. It feels like a place from a different time—the past, certainly, but also perhaps a future. There's not much plastic around (a couple of rain barrels) and few of the bright colours of modern life. A lot
of wood, both in the buildings and the air; the smell of pine and wood
smoke hangs in the haze. It's also exceptionally quiet. Really, exactly the
sort of environs you'd expect to feature a shaman (but rather convenient
for the shops). The last cabin on the left is where I find her.

Annette (the shaman) welcomes me in. It's a cosy place: a single room with a high bed in one corner, a small kitchen in the other, a wood-burning stove, and various bits of dead animal dotted around (a pair of wings "from an eagle," she tells me, a pair of antlers from a deer). I take a seat in a rocking chair next to the stove while Annette makes us some tea. She has long, white hair and black eyes and a face with some deep wrinkles. She puts me slightly in mind of a witch, but a (mostly) good witch. Her cabin really makes me feel like I've stepped one thousand miles north and one hundred years sideways, rather than just off a Copenhagen street.

I'm somewhat encumbered by my technology. I have three digital recording devices aimed at us; their blinking red lights seem quite out of place. Annette requests that I turn them all off, but after some negotiation we compromise on leaving just the one running. When we're settled with tea and crackers, she sits down on the opposite side of the small wooden table and asks me, in her Scandinavian-tinged accent, why I've sought her out.

I explain that I'm supposed to be becoming an elephant, but it's not going all that well, and that I was talking to my friend in a pub who had done a shamanic journey and she suggested I try to do one, too, to see if it'll help with my project…

"And, in summary, I was hoping you could send me to the spirit world to meet my power animal?"

She sighs. For reasons of her own, she's not going to help me undertake a shamanic journey to retrieve my power animal. For that I will have to go elsewhere. However, she can clearly see that my trying to become an elephant is, as she puts it bluntly, "idiotic."

Idiotic. That takes the wind out of my sails. "Oh. Why?" I ask.

"Well, what have you got to do with the elephants? Nothing. They're completely alien to the environment you're connected to. If you were a bushman in Africa, then yes, an elephant would be possible. But you are not a bushman, and you're from London. You could only get closer to an animal that's near to you in terms of your shared environment, the places you live in and move through."

"But we have elephants in England—in zoos," I protest.

She dismisses my pedantry: "They are all mad, though."

I have to agree. I tell her I took a vow to never again visit a zoo after taking my girlfriend to Wilhelma zoo in Stuttgart for our second and, as it's turned out, second-worst date. The place was simply bursting with animals driven insane by their captivity, including a pair of elephants, who endlessly performed the same sequence of stereotyped motions.

"So what animals do you have in London *apart* from in zoos? You have Fox. You have Deer."

Deer we have: half of bloody London used to be the stag-hunting grounds of the aristocracy, and a few herds remain in Greenwich Park, formerly hunted by King Henry VIII.

"You are much closer to Deer in terms of the connection through the environment." She sizes me up. "In fact, Deer is still too wild for you. Really…the Sheep."

A pause, during which she considers me more carefully.

"Actually, for you, the Goat."

A goat. Yes…a goat!

A wave of relief and gratitude floods over me. Relief because of narrowly avoiding being proclaimed a sheep. Gratitude because with a goat I *know* Annette has gotten it absolutely right. A goat—a goat is so much more my level. Sure, elephants have conveniently short necks, but what *connection* do I have with them? I mean, just in practical terms it took a once-in-a-lifetime opportunity and a journey across half the world to see them in their natural environment. In contrast, there is a herd of goats just down the flipping road from where I live.

I know. It's a massive cliché: I sought out a shaman about an uncertainty and she told me to stick to my dream. Because, gentle reader, there is a dream mixed up in this project, too, or rather, should I say, a vision, half-remembered from when I was very small.

The vision goes like this: there is a leafy houseplant, which one day I decide to eat. But it's the manner of eating that I particularly remember, because I decide to eat it without using my hands. I remember tugging at a leafy branch with my teeth. The stem resisting, the bush rustling…

I throw my head back determinedly, and the stem snaps off in my mouth, and I begin to chew the leaves.

I'm not sure how old I am in this short snippet of internal video, but eating this houseplant without my hands was evidently such a profound feeling, it has stuck with me all these years.

Annette in her wisdom has released me from the elephant that I had arrived at oh, so logically (well, sort of) and without knowing it told me to stick to the dream! Would an elephant tug at a branch with its teeth? No. It would use its armlike trunk. Would an elephant gallop across a landscape? Impossible, because elephants physically cannot gallop! But a goat? Check and check!

Goat.

Annette demonstrating the deer dance in her kitchen.

Annette wastes no time getting down to brass tacks.

"So how could you be a nonhuman being, in this case an animal? Well, now, there are old ways, ritual and magic and spiritual ways it's done within shamanic tradition. And one thing is, you get the outer form, the movement, and you start by imitating that. So there are some peoples, like the Pueblo people of the southwestern United States, who would have half the skull of the deer, with the antlers. You put them on—"

Annette rises from the table and starts sort of swinging her head with imaginary antlers from side to side.

"—and you feel the weight… And then you have two sticks."

She holds her arms out in front of her, hands grasping the tops of two imaginary deer-leg sticks, and begins rhythmically stepping with them around the kitchen, demonstrating this deer dance and explaining: "So you become four-legged. And there are even hooves on the end of the legs. And so you start this honouring magic, calling Deer in a spirit dance."

She steps over to her mantelpiece and picks up a short stick with black beads tied to one end—a rattle. She starts rattling as she continues moving around the kitchen.

"This is also a way of doing it…of becoming one with the spirit of an animal. A rattle with this sort of lightness of sound…The lightness of a beautiful animal."

She continues to dance around the kitchen, rhythmically shaking her rattle, and starts to hum deeply but then abruptly breaks out of it, returning to sit at the table and handing me the rattle to inspect.

"These rattles are used all over the world. I have much bigger rattles, from the stag and the reindeer, which make a deeper sound, but these are the hooves of a row deer." She's referring to the beads tied to the end of the rattle.

"Every one of these is like a fingernail, and there was a bone I had to pull out. Like the tip of the finger."

"Gruesome."

"Well, it was my Christmas Eve project."

Annette continues: "So in a way, it starts through cold imitation. But then you can enter into this 'between-the-worlds state,' or 'trans-ecstasy,'

The earliest known drawing of a Siberian shaman, from the 1692 book *Noord en Oost Tartarije*, an account by the Dutch explorer Nicolaas Witsen of his travels in Siberia. It portrays an Evenk shaman, performing a ritual with a drum, and is labeled "een Schaman ofte Duyvel-priester" (Shaman or Devil-Priest).

Hunters' or Deer Dance, painted circa 1932 by Alphonso Roybal.

San Juan Pueblo deer dance, photographed circa 1977 by Richard Erdoes.

or 'changed state of consciousness.'" She waves the words aside to imply the term itself is unimportant. "But because you have called and honoured the spirit of Deer, you can then *experience* this transformation, seeing the world through the eyes of the animal."

She leans back in her chair, concluding: "So, that sort of changed state of consciousness is *pretty* helpful."

"Right, yes." I'm nodding and agreeing, but I'm wondering how I'm going to enter into a state of trans-ecstasy without visiting one of London's more insalubrious nightclubs. She continues: "However. These people *know* the animal. They have been following and watching and remembering the life and the way of it their whole lives. *It's in their bones.* So I don't know how much it will work if you have *no* knowledge of the animal."

I'm a little offended by her emphasis on the word *no*, because surely I have *some* knowledge of "the animal." But when I come to think of it, I do see many more dead (bits of) animal than living ones in any given week. A walk through the supermarket and there are lots of bits of dead animal from a variety of species, whereas a walk through the park? Well, some pigeons and a few dogs. I did a quick survey. Number of animal species represented in my local supermarket: twenty-nine. Number of animal species I see in a trip to my local park: two. Including *homo sapiens*.

So Annette's summing up my knowledge of animals—me being someone who has lived in cities my entire life—as essentially nil in comparison with people who have grown up tracking and hunting them is perhaps fair (though I'm not that happy about this newly realised lack of nonhuman animal contact; I resolve to get a cat). In fact, that's what Annette does professionally sometimes—she tries to "reconnect city people to their hunter-gatherer souls." And, she tells me, "they take to it like ducks to water."

Our conversation continues, and Annette digs out a photograph of a shaman from Siberia doing an antelope dance (my notion that shamanism is a "Native American thing" has been corrected; the word originally comes from Siberia and is now used to describe similar practices found in cultures indigenous to every part of the globe). I comment on the fact that the photograph's date is almost a hundred years old. Annette fixes me with a look.

"People have been trying to bridge the gap between animal and human always. *Always.*"

And it seems she's quite right.

* * *

In 1939 a German geologist named Otto Völzing was helping with the excavation of the Hohlenstein-Stadel cave in the Swabian Alps in southern Germany. The excavations had been successful, and Völzing had dug up the skeletons of thirty-eight Stone Age people as well as the skulls of a man, woman, and child. For some long-lost reason, their heads had been severed and buried at the entrance of the cave, all arranged staring towards the southwest. The dig, funded by the Nazi SS to find evidence for their belief that human civilisation started in Germany, was cut short by the start of the Second World War. Völzing was called up to fight, but on his last day he found a whole bunch of fragments of ivory buried deep in the very back of the cave. These he diligently packed up in a box before going off to fight the Allies.

The box of tusk shards ended up in a local museum and was forgotten. It wasn't until 1969 that someone doing an inventory realised that the shards were woolly mammoth tusk and actually the remains of a statuette. The figure that emerged as the fragments were pieced together was a carving of a human figure with a lion's head, and the latest dating techniques show it was carved forty thousand years ago. This makes it the oldest nonabstract art and the oldest figurative sculpture in existence, and it's a human-animal hybrid.

While we can't know why it was carved, it's clear it took a lot of work; a sculptor recently tried to make an (elephant) ivory copy using only the type of flint tools that were around forty thousand years ago, and it took him almost three months of solid work. This effort means it must have been important to the makers. So while it could have been a toy or something (the Lion Human does seem smiley to me), by far its most likely purpose was as some kind of spiritual talisman.

Der Löwenmensch ("the Lion Human") of
Hohlenstein-Stadel, carved 40,000 years ago and
the oldest work of figurative art yet found.

Representations of human-animal hybrids have been found painted
in the deepest parts of other caves frequented by people living during the
Upper Palaeolithic (the end of the Stone Age). For example, there are
the paintings in the Chauvet Cave in the Ardèche Gorge in France. This
cave, stumbled into by three spelunkers in the early 1990s, had until that
moment been sealed off for 25,000 years. It contains hundreds of paintings of animals, but in the deepest chamber there's a figure of a half-hu-
man, half-bison that was painted by a person 30,000 years ago. Also, in a
cave in Lascaux, France, there's a painting of a man (he has an erection)
with a bird's head, lying on the floor, that is 16,500 years old. And there's
the so-called Sorcerer painting from around 13,000 years ago in the Trois
Frères Cave in Ariège, France, showing a man with antlers, dancing.

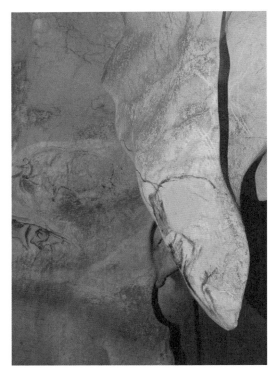

The bison-headed human painted 30,000 years ago on a rock pendant deep in the Chauvet Cave.

Bird-headed man with a bird-headed staff, lying (dying?) in front of a bison that seems to have been disembowelled by a spear.

The art at Trois Frères Cave is difficult to make out in photographs,
as it's engraved into the rock as well as drawn with charcoal. The discoverer of the cave
made sketches of the cave art, though. Top: The Sorcerer figure with antlers and tail.
Below: A bison-headed man playing a nose flute.

All these examples are from a small patch of Europe. It was once thought that the Stone Age Europeans invented the practice of sculpting and painting figures (with the implication that the cognitive and cultural beginnings of creativity were in Le Europe, reinforcing the nineteenth-century idea that Europeans and their descendants are exceptional). But this Eurocentric view seems to have been more due to the fact that the conditions in Europe have been right for preservation and, more important, study: only in 2014 did a scientist do the work to accurately test the age of some cave paintings of animals in Indonesia. She found them to be 35 to 39,000 years old, the same age as the oldest paintings in Europe. The temporal concurrence yet wide geographic separation of these similar Indonesian and European paintings suggests that the practice likely started before the populations who spread east towards Indonesia and west into Europe diverged from North Africa around 60,000 years ago.

Who knows when a person actually first imagined being a lion-man or a bison-man or a bird-man (or, for that matter, a goat-man)? But as the cave paintings and figurines are thought to represent the beliefs people had about the world before history—our first attempts at answering the eternal questions Who am I? Why am I here? and Where do I go?—it's likely people have been trying to bridge the gap between humans and other animals for a bloody long time, if not, as Annette said, *always*. So really, to want to become a goat is pretty standard. In fact, historically speaking, it's almost odder to *not* want to become a goat.

*　*　*

I ask Annette why a shaman would want to transform into an animal, anyway.

She tells me that shamanism originates from when we were all hunters and gatherers, surviving on whatever we could find or kill. A shaman would try to become one with an animal in order to track and hunt it.

But it's also an animist worldview. In this system it's not just humans who can have a soul or who are considered persons; animals are very much people, too. This presents a bit of a conundrum for the shamanic hunter because if you're hunting and killing and eating an animal and an animal is a person, well, you're engaging in murder and cannibalism. So another reason a shaman would want to become an animal is to ask forgiveness from the animal spirit for killing it. This seems a little bit paradoxical from my point of view.

"So part of this becoming an animal is to sort of lessen your guilt?" I ask Annette, seeking clarification.

"Well, it's like you recognise they are your kin. They are your relatives, and we have an ongoing agreement. Hunting is a pact. And in order for Deer to allow itself to be met and killed, you have to pay your honours by right behaviour, and part of this is to become the prey. But you have to fulfil your part. Humans aren't doing that."

She tells me about a people, the Yukaghirs, who to this day are practicing shamans and hunters in Siberia: "These hunters try and take the humanness off themselves and become one with the animal, so they can think like the animal and track it."

She refers me to a book, *Soul Hunters*, by the anthropologist Rane Willerslev, who (partly to escape being murdered by the Siberian authorities) lived and hunted with a group of Yukaghirs for eighteen months deep in the forests of Siberia. In his book Willerslev describes a hunter called Old Spiridon, who hunted elk dressed in elk fur, with elk ears on his hat and the skin from the legs of an elk covering his skis, so he'd sound like an elk moving through the snow. Willerslev was with Old Spiridon as he closed in on an elk and her calf and watched as he began moving and acting like his prey to such an extent that the "female elk…captured by his mimetic performance, suspended her disbelief and started walking straight towards him." Then Old Spiridon shot it and its calf dead. This is all very logical and easy to comprehend: "becoming" an elk clearly helps with killing elks, just as calling like a duck helps with killing ducks. What's less easy is Old Spiridon's description of the encounter. He said that he was seeing the elk as "a beautiful young woman, beckoning to me.…If I'd gone with them, I would have died myself, at which point I shot them both." Not only did Old Spiridon become an elk, the elk at the same time became a human. For Annette and the Yukaghirs and the other shamanic peoples of the world, the divisions between human and nonhuman are much more flexible than I'm used to.

When faced with a story like Old Spiridon's, the Western–born and bred like me will say that he's making it up for effect, and if he's not making it up, then he must just be delusional. Or, if we're adopting a more modern, respectful-of-different-cultures approach, we'll say, "Ahhhh, the wise one must be speaking in metaphor: he means it's *as if* the elk became a woman or the shaman became *like* a goat. And when the lying/delusional/wise primitive insists that no, he's not speaking in metaphor and that the elk *was* a woman and, yes, the shaman *became* a goat, we smile and nod and say, "Yes, of course, wise one," and then, sotto voce, "They haven't quite got the concept of metaphor yet, though, huh?"

Now, I'm rather scientifically inclined and not one to elevate ancient belief systems as necessarily more in tune with the natural world. For instance, when the ancient Aborigines reached Australia, they hunted 60 percent of the large mammals to extinction.[3] However, I'm also trying to become a goat, and, furthermore, Annette, a shamanic practitioner, is kind and smart and doesn't seem delusional or primitive or intellectually unsophisticated. She does have a very different view from mine of what animals and people *are,* though.

Willerslev asks: What if we just consider the possibility that these shamanic people mean what they say when they say they can become animals and animals can become people? I think he's on to something. I mean, two groups of people looking at exactly the same situation and coming to wildly different conclusions, both of which are correct depending on underlying assumptions held about the world—that's never happened before, right? Willerslev goes on to trace the difference of opinion as to the transmutability of humans and animals back to different underlying philosophies as to what constitutes being a person.

Now, gentle reader, I'm not a professional philosopher, so if you are, I suggest you just close your eyes for the next few paragraphs because I

---

3 And overhunting by Yukaghirs has led to the decline of the elk populations in their area. Not that there's many buffalo left in the USA, or bears in the UK, for that matter.

think I'm about to wade in and bludgeon in most gruesome fashion a discourse that has been continuing for hundreds of years across thousands of pages of philosophical treatise. And with that caveat…

Willerslev in his book argues that for Western-educated minds like mine, the underlying assumptions one holds about one's self and other selves are still profoundly influenced by the philosophy of René Descartes and his famous thought experiment described in his book *Meditations on First Philosophy,* published way back in 1641.

The story goes that Descartes, sitting by the fire one night, asked himself: What can I know for sure? All of the reality I think I experience could be an illusion perpetrated by a malignant demon. Or, to bring it up to date: We could all just be in a big computer simulation, dude. Although it *seems* that I'm sitting in a chair by a fire, how do I know it exists? I could be dreaming, or I could just be a weird disembodied mind somewhere, somehow being fed the illusion that I've got a body and that there's a chair it's sitting in. I can doubt everything; how do I know I even exist? From this methodical doubting of existence, Descartes tries to establish a solid foundation for some certainty. He reasons that there's one thing at least he can be certain of, and that is that there's something doing all this doubting. All of physical reality could be an illusion, but in order to have that doubtful thought, some thinking must be happening, and therefore the "I" that's doing the thinking has got to exist: *Cogito ergo sum.* I think; therefore I am.

Having established this one certainty in an otherwise doubtful world, he goes on to argue that one's mind, the I, *must* be a different thing from one's body. This is because two things need to have the same essential properties to be the same. Descartes argues that while it's easy to conceive of dividing a physical thing like a body or a pencil into parts, he can't "distinguish any parts" within his mind; the mind is "something quite single and complete." Therefore, the body is essentially divisible, and the mind is essentially indivisible, and because one thing can't have both these contradictory properties, the mind and the body must be separate.

So Descartes managed to elevate reason as the fundamental characteristic required for something to have a self, and to separate the reasoning mind from the physical body. Conveniently, if you're a Christian, as Descartes was, the argument that the mind and body are different plays nicely with the notion that a person has an eternal soul that, after the death of the body, can separate and go to heaven. Furthermore, Descartes argues that because animals can't reason (they couldn't think: *I* think therefore *I* am), they can't be conscious. So they're effectively just biological automata, and any of their cries of pain or what have you can be ignored as being purely mechanical, like the chimes of a clock (Descartes was a pioneer of vivisection).

His classic bit of reasoning has become known as Cartesian dualism, and dualism in various forms has had a pretty big effect on Western science and philosophy—mind versus body, reason versus instinct, civilisation versus savagery, humanity versus animality, objectivity versus subjectivity—and these dichotomies have been causing no end of problems ever since. But for our present purpose the important implications are that animals don't have consciousness and, more fundamentally, our own consciousness is independent of the physical world.

But now we turn to the philosopher Martin Heidegger. Join me as I swim so far out of intellectual depth I'll be at risk of drowning.

The phenomenological alternative to Cartesian dualism, elaborated in the 1960s by Heidegger, among others, turns Descartes on his head. For one, Heidegger points out that it's actually not possible to think without thinking *about* something: Descartes's "I think; therefore I am" should actually be "I think *about something*; therefore I am." While one of the things we can think and reason about is our own mind, we can think about plenty of other things, too. And that opens a crack: What makes thinking about your own thoughts more fundamental than thinking thoughts that make up other aspects of your perceived existence? Heidegger basically rejects the idea that the fundamental aspect of your being, your I, is a mind that can reason.

Sure, when we're pontificating about ourselves, we might reason that our mind could be disembodied or that it looks out from just behind our eyes (at the pineal gland in the centre of the brain is where Descartes imagined it), making decisions and telling our body to do things. But this rational consideration is just one mode of thinking, which for the most part doesn't reflect what it's like to exist anyway. After all, we can only work from the evidence available, and I don't know about you, but my moment-to-moment existence is bumbling along as things momentarily capture my attention: oh, a little itch on my nose; uncross and recross my legs; oh, look, a lady; back to work; this chair *is* uncomfortable; scratch my nose; hold on, this is freaking me out; I've got to remember to breathe! Oh wait, phew, breathing happens automatically. It's funny, that, when you think about it.

Voilà, bumbling along—a mixed bag of sensations that when it's feeling philosophical *can* reason abstractly like Descartes, but at a more fundamental level is inescapably and inseparably, as Heidegger calls us, a "being-in-the-world."

So how does this relate to people becoming goats and goats becoming people? Well, according to the phenomenological view, our selves exist as a result of our interactions with the world. Willerslev argues that the Yukaghirs, rather than having a Cartesian view of a person as a self-contained mind that isn't fundamentally dependent on the external physical world, the Yukaghirs take a more phenomenological view. Rather than viewing their selves being independent discrete minds, they think of themselves as so dependent on their physical context that what they are is constructed by where they are and what they're doing. This also helps explain the importance of setting for shamanic rituals. So when shamans change their behaviour and physicality by mimicking an animal, they are changing their context; and since what you are depends on your context, if you change your context radically enough you can actually move towards becoming that animal. Willerslev writes that the Yukaghirs are actually careful not to go *too* far in changing their body and behaviour because of the danger of fully becoming that animal, from which apparently there is no return.

It's quite difficult for me to imagine myself really believing I've become a goat, or rather (my mistake) *actually* becoming a goat by changing how I behave and how I move. It's just not how I've been brought up. But if Old Spiridon, through his behaviour, managed to change his relationship to the world so much that the female elk didn't see him as a dangerous human hunter anymore, and he saw the elk as a human in turn, well, for a moment, the elk and the person were also the person and the elk. As the Yukaghirs point out to Willerslev, from the elk's point of view, *it's* the person.

This is the profound shift in perspective I need to try to achieve with my project. If I'm to experience the world as a goat, I need to change my context in the world to the extent that somehow I look at a chair and don't automatically associate it with sitting. That I look at a word and don't automatically read it. That I look at a(nother) goat and think of it as another person, like me.

*   *   *

Before I leave Annette's cabin to go and teach my master class, she has a final word on my project. She advises me to try to go further into "this mystical, spiritual process of honouring the animal and calling for its spirit." She's sure, however, that in the end I'll have "to peel off the mysticality of it" because, she thinks, what I've set out to do, trying to use technology to get closer to nature, is a paradox: "No one would get such a crazy idea like this fifty years ago. This estrangement from nature has gone to completely idiotic extremes already, and it continues down the abyss."

"Our technology is changing us. That's without doubt," I say.

"You have to decide if your project is really about trying to make a costume, or is the most important thing trying to find a way for people to feel their kinship, to bridge the gap, to feel like an animal? Because then you're gonna do everything much simpler. Then it's the mystical thing. Then it's an education."

*   *   *

Back in London a couple of weeks later (everyone said the master class was probably one of the greatest examples of pedagogy in the history of design, by the way), I decide to go a little further into the spiritual aspect of shamanism and sign up myself and, after some persuasion, my friend Simon for a Saturday workshop in Newport, Wales, called

"An Introduction to Shamanic Journeying." Simon is an old friend, and though he's not keen on Wales as a place to visit (childhood trauma), he does appreciate the odd foray into unreality, and we've been helping each other with our various more or less absurd projects since we were teenagers. On the way there we both decide to approach the day with an open mind (and I make Simon swear that he'll not mercilessly ridicule anyone). We've been asked to bring a cushion, a blindfold, and a blanket so that we'll be comfortable when we're journeying, which makes me think we could be "away" for some time. I'm very much hoping that my animal helper spirit will be Goat (and if not Goat, then maybe something cool like Eagle or Cheetara).

The Newport Clinic of Holistic Health is a terraced red-brick house just off the M4 motorway, and the workshop is to be held in the meeting room. Our fellow shamanic initiates are six ladies ranging in age from nose-studded student to late-middle-aged mother of grown-up children. I get the impression that a couple of group members are here to try and deal with personal tragedy, as I overhear them talking to Maxine, our group leader, showing her objects they've been given special dispensation to bring along to help with contacting specific spirits in the land of the dead.

The chairs are cleared to one side, and once we're all sat on our cushions in a circle, Maxine takes us through the basics of shamanic journeying on the whiteboard, helping us choose our personal *axis mundi* and so on. Your *axis mundi* is a place that you know well, that becomes your gateway from ordinary reality into nonordinary reality. The place you go to in your mind to climb up to the upper world or dig down to the lower world. A tree from one's childhood garden is a "very good one, Thomas." The day wears on, with Maxine telling us at some length her own personal story of how she was chosen to become a shamanic practitioner, until finally, in the late afternoon, we get to try journeying ourselves. We lie back on our cushions, I shut my eyes, and Maxine starts banging her drum, a fast intense rhythm, and I imagine my *axis mundi* and dig down into the roots, and down and down and down and, well, it sort of works…

I see some patterns and start to hear a kind of heavenly harmonic singing, and then, as though it's lit by flickering flames, appearing and disappearing in and out of the shadows…It's kind of ghostly and difficult to fixate on and almost abstract, but it's definitely…a rabbit. It dances in and out of patterns of light and dark, and it never stops to talk to me or tell me what I should do, but it's *definitely* there flitting in and out of the flickering shadows. Just appearing and disappearing and kind of leaping and flying through the darkness. The beat of the drum gets louder and faster and then abruptly softens, and I hear Maxine calling us back to the world. I'm not sure how long I've been in nonordinary reality, maybe fifteen minutes, but our journeying session is at an end. After we all gradually sit up and let our eyes readjust to the room, we go around the circle and relate what we saw in our visions. Some of us didn't manage anything. Stud-nosed girl *supposedly* went on an epic adventure, rriding on the back of a dragon deep into the land of the dead and then into space to discuss the state of the world with some lizard aliens and then flying to heaven to meet God or *whatever* (overachiever). When it's my turn, I tell of my simple visitation by Rabbit and the heavenly singing. Maxine is pleased. I'm quite pleased, too; OK, it wasn't Goat, but at least I was visited by a Spirit. When it's Simon's turn, strangely, Simon has also received a visit from Rabbit. That is odd. But what could it mean? Maxine can't explain it either, but says it likely has some significance for our future work together.

Maxine can't explain it either, but says it likely has some significance for our future work together.

Maxine can't explain it either. After looking into everyone's eyes in turn to check that we have *fully* returned from nonordinary reality and are back in our bodies and thus are safe to drive, she sends us on our way with the warning to not try journeying without the aid of a shamanic professional.

As we set off back to London, I ask Simon what he thought about us both seeing visions of Rabbit.

"Er…You didn't get that it's from *Watership Down*?"

Oh…Ah, yes. I remember. It seems our visions both drew quite heavily on a sequence from a childhood cartoon that featured a ghostly rabbit.

"And the heavenly singing you told everyone you hallucinated was just Maxine."

Oh... *Maxine* was singing, and I was hearing it through my ears, not from the spirit world? Oh, I suppose that would make more sense. She's a pretty wonderful singer, though.

"You knob end," says Simon.

* * *

Feeling decidedly uncomfortable after our brush with the Welsh neo-shamanic scene, I decide that perhaps I should take a head-on approach to this issue of altered perception. Annette hadn't mentioned it, and Maxine skirted around the issue, but we all know that psychoactive substances are among the tools used at shamanic ceremonies. And so, gentle reader, I *may or may not* have found myself in possession of certain plant matter, which *may or may not* have given rise to the very worst experience of my life, crashing headfirst through the doors of perception and blundering around like an absolute lunatic, upsetting the furniture and everyone else, for that matter. And no, I'm pretty sure I didn't get any closer to the experience of what it might be like to be a goat—unless being a goat involves being extremely freaked out and the world going all weird and geometric and getting locked out of your house in the rain with no wallet, no phone, no keys, and no shoes or socks. Which, let me tell you, is not a happy situation, because having bare feet in the rain makes you look like a total nut job, which means people are even less inclined to help you, especially if you're wild eyed and don't know what it is you actually want helping with. Using drugs of all kinds (both legal and illegal) to find relief from the anguish or the boredom or the worry of existence is a big part of human existence: getting out of one's head, off one's face and such, looking to alter one's perception. But for me, in this case, I didn't find relief at all. In fact, my worries and fears were epically magnified. I eventually convinced a taxi driver to take me to my girlfriend's house. It was not fun... And that's all I've got to say about that (except: kids, be *extremely* wary of strongly hallucinogenic plant matter).

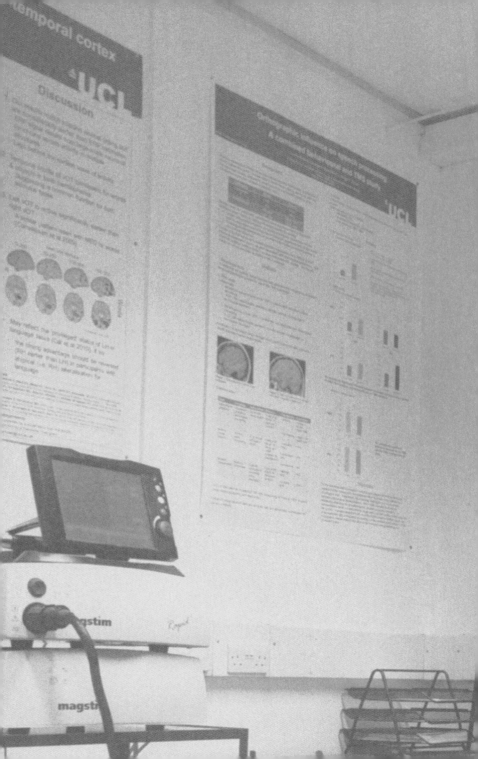

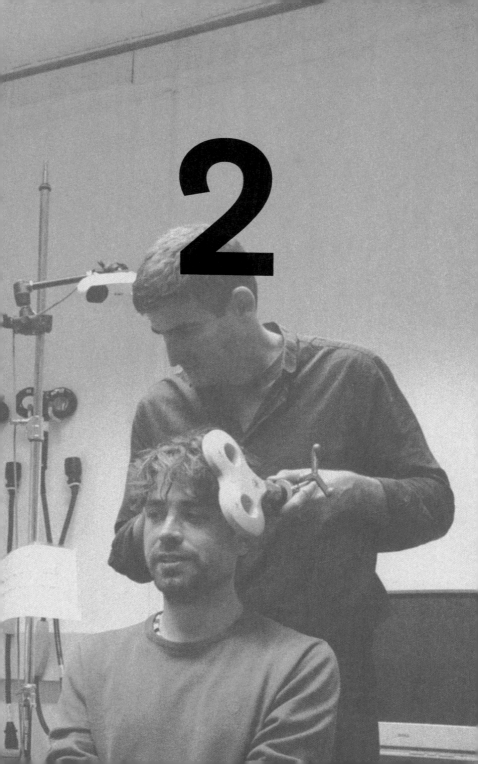

Mind

Buttercups Sanctuary for Goats
(a bright new day)

I need to get back to reality and approach the problem of goat perception from solid scientific bedrock. And who better to ask about the mental life of goats than Britain's foremost goat behaviour expert, Dr. Alan McElligott?[1]

He and his PhD students study the goats at Buttercups, the United Kingdom's (if not the world's) only sanctuary for abused goats, which happens to be located just down the road from where I live.

Visiting Buttercups is so exciting. There are goats everywhere! Wandering around the yard, butting heads, eating, clanging their horns against the metal feeding troughs just for the sheer joy of it, standing on things, sitting on things, chewing on things, pooing on things...doing all the things goats like to do. Buttercups Sanctuary for Goats is heaven on Earth for goatkind, or at least a luxury spa resort. If you're a goat at Buttercups, upon waking in your own warm and comfortable stall (which you can have all to yourself or enjoy with a close companion or two), you

---

1 Dr. McElligott's goat expertise has more to do with pragmatics than an overriding passion for goats. As an ethologist (a scientist who studies animal behaviour), he's chosen to work with goats because they're neophilic. That is, when presented with a novel situation (like the specially constructed equipment he uses in various experiments), they're less inclined to just ignore the experiment and cower in the corner than, say, sheep. This curiosity makes them interesting from a cognitive point of view and easier to study.

Chatting with Bob and the goats at Buttercups.

A happy goat?

will be presented with a breakfast specially prepared to your individual tastes and requirements. After breakfast, the day is your own, and you're free to amble about the yard enjoying the attention of the staff (grooming, pedicures, and the best medical care money can buy) or to laze on the various structures provided for your enrichment. Or, if you're a more active and competitive spirit, why not see if you can climb the highest and become king (or queen) atop The Mound? And, of course, there's always roaming in the fields of fresh green grass, dappled with the flowers that give your home its name, *buttercups*. When I'm a goat, I want to go to Buttercups before I die.

I meet Bob, the founder of Buttercups ("I started with two goats; now I've got two hundred fifty"), who regales me with tales of goats and introduces me to his general manager, Gower, and some of the volunteers who look after these animals. It seems a good place, and, as Gower confides later (after we witness some eccentric human behaviour from a couple of the volunteers), "It's a sanctuary for humans, too."

Dr. Alan McElligott: goat expert.

My meeting with Dr. McElligott takes place back in his office at Queen Mary University. On the wall he has a framed edition of the prestigious journal *Proceedings of the Royal Society B* with an image of one of his very own test subjects on the front.

"Yeah, we got the cover," he says all casually in his Irish accent. This is a man with impeccable goat credentials.

I want to find out about goat behaviour for obvious reasons. The reasons are not obvious to Dr. McElligott, however. We begin at the beginning.

"Why do you want to be a goat?" he asks.

"Well, I went to see a shaman, and she told me to be a goat."

"Oh, right. I see," says Dr. McElligott. After a pause, he continues: "Why did you go to see a shaman?"

"Well, I just got pretty glum about trying to become an elephant."

"Right, of course," says Dr. McElligott. Is that a resigned glance at the clock on the wall as I settle down at his desk?

"Dare I ask: Why did you want to become an elephant?"

"Ah, yes…Well, I think I was just feeling the weight of the world as a human and thought: Wouldn't it be better to be an animal for a while? So I wouldn't have to worry about, you know, human worries."

"*Riiight.*"

"So I was wondering: Do goats worry?"

"Yes."

Shit.

Thankfully, Dr. McElligott has more to say on the subject: "Actually, I wouldn't call it *worry*. They get anxious—stressed, perhaps. We know this from an experiment we did with the goats at Buttercups to try to identify emotions, where we put heart monitors on them, equipment to record vocalisations, tail posture, ear posture, and so on. And then we put the goats in a 'negative state.'"

Dr. McElligott is then very careful to emphasise that they "always work ethically" and "the goats are never in any danger, as that wouldn't be ethical." And if they *do* put the animals under stress, anything they do, they do "for less than five minutes," and so on. His assurances have the opposite effect on me, and I'm sort of braced for some kind of *Clockwork Orange*–type experiment, but with goats.

Dr. McElligott goes on: "The experiment we do is what's called a 'food frustration' experiment. Basically, we feed a goat in one pen while letting a goat in the adjacent pen watch. So the goat that isn't getting the food is put in a negative state. But without it being extremely stressful. As that wouldn't be ethical."

Dr. McElligott and the ethics committee have considered the ethics of making a goat slightly jealous and concluded that in the name of science, it would not be unethical. As long as the goat is jealous for less than five minutes.

"When you listen to goats, it all sounds quite monotonous. But there are in fact subtle changes in their bleats and slight shifts in ear and tail posture, depending on whether they're in a neutral, negative, or even slightly positive state."

So…goats are capable of getting a bit stressed and sound a bit different when they do. I don't want to seem ungrateful to Dr. McElligott and his colleagues, but this is hardly the profound sort of insight into goat minds I was hoping for. But as we talk, I start to understand where Dr. McElligott is coming from. As an ethologist, he's interested in saying things about animal minds with a degree of certainty (and a quantified degree of certainty, at that). This is an extremely hard thing to do. It's hard enough working out what's going on in another person's mind given all the benefits of being a person yourself, and even *with* words, we get it wrong. With animals, not only can you not ask what they're thinking, you can't really even draw on your own experience. Because how do you *know* what it's like to be an animal? Therein lies the difficulty of the ethologist: if you want to say for sure what an animal thinks, well, you have to get the animal to somehow *demonstrate* what it's thinking.

As an analogy, I can imagine a scientist from a species of strange aliens with different ways of perceiving the world and communicating. The scientist, starting from the reasonable assumption that I wouldn't like being hit on the head, experimentally hits me on the head and notes the changing tone of the sounds I make, my narrowing eyes, and the scrunching up of my forehead and concludes that's how *Homo sapiens sapiens* react when put in a negative state. ("Hey, Zarg, turns out they *don't* like your tickle probe.")

When we watch a video of some cute baby goats springing about all over the place in sheer *joy* because they've just been let out of their shed for the spring, I say, "Ahhhh, those goats are so happy!" Dr. McElligott cautions me to be more cautious. "You can be anthropomorphic and say they're happy. But we need to study that scientifically to be able to identify it, not just assume. So what I'd say is this is an indication that they really vocalise a lot when they're in an excited state." In fact, throughout the conversation, he refuses to use phrases that anthropomorphise the goats in any way.

Dr. McElligott and Annette are polar opposites in their approach to the inner life of animals. Annette starts by endowing animals with all the aspects of personhood, whereas Dr. McElligott works from the assumption that they have none. However, I suspect that their underlying goals aren't too dissimilar in terms of reassessing the contemporary human-nonhuman animal contract, because much of Dr. McElligott's work is relevant to improving the welfare of the billions of nonhuman animals farmed as livestock.

He tells me about an experiment they did at Buttercups to investigate whether goats that arrived at the sanctuary from abusive homes exhibited a "negative cognitive bias": that is, were they in a glass-half-empty frame of mind? Presented with an ambiguous stimulus, like a little corridor of a kind that they'd previously been trained to expect to have a tasty goat treat at the end only half the time, would they choose to walk down the corridor and have a look (glass half-full) or avoid it (glass half-empty)? By walking down the corridor or not, the goats thus revealed their mood to the ethologist peeking at them with clipboard in hand.

Buttercups is a sanctuary both in name and by nature. Many of the goats there have been rescued from more or less horribly unfortunate circumstances. When we arrived at the sanctuary, Bob told us some genuine horror stories. One goat, named Lucky, had been found in a pond by a member of the public. Its throat had been slit and tail cut off, and it had been left to drown. Amazingly, it survived and was brought to Buttercups: hence, Lucky. They thought another goat had black hair when it was brought in, but it turned out it was covered in diesel. It is called Diesel. Tales of humans abusing goats abound at Buttercups (there's Curry and Bobbin, too). Dr. McElligott's results showed that after at least two years of good care at Buttercups, goats rescued from abusive homes didn't exhibit a negative cognitive bias compared to those that hadn't been abused. In fact, female goats rescued from abusive homes were even slightly more positive than their nonabused counterparts, possibly suggesting long-term optimism after escaping their abusers.

In human equivalents of Dr. McElligott's ambiguous-corridor experiment, some people exhibit a negative cognitive bias. This strongly correlates with their suffering from "low mood" and (if persistent) clinical depression (as gauged from their questionnaire answers).[2] If goats outwardly show a negative cognitive bias, can we infer that inwardly they're feeling low or even depressed? It would seem pretty churlish to deny

---

2 You could actually say "less positive" as opposed to "negative" cognitive bias, because experiments have suggested that people with mild depression are actually more realistic about their chances in life. For example, they are less likely to think buying that lottery ticket is worthwhile and more likely to think that yes, they might be the one in the one in three who will get cancer.

goats emotions if equivalent behaviour in humans is accepted as indicating they're feeling sad.

The cognitive bias experiment is in one form or another a commonly used way of getting around the fact that animals can't tell you how they're feeling (no surveys for goats along the lines of "In the past month, how often have you avoided social situations?"). Experiments have been done with sheep, dogs, rats, starlings, and little chicks. And after they've been subjected to various forms of (I'm sure ethically considered) stressful situations, all have shown a negative cognitive bias, so we can attribute internal emotional states to them, too. Animals other than ourselves show negative cognitive biases and therefore can feel sad. Not hugely surprising when we're talking about goats or dogs or rats, but what about bees? Can a bee be depressed or at least have negative emotions? Because bees show cognitive biases, too. I asked one of the scientists who conducted the research on bees' biases, Dr. Geraldine Wright of Newcastle University, what she thinks of this. Her reply was that it is "logically inconsistent to attribute emotions to goats and other animals on the basis of cognitive bias experiments and not bees." So maybe there are some bees sadly buzzing around out there—or maybe demonstrating a negative cognitive bias isn't in fact analogous to saying "I'm feeling sad."

The fact that even the most basic of feelings are difficult to scientifically pin down in animals illustrates just how hard it is to say anything definite about what's going on in their minds. It's one reason why ethologists like Dr. McElligott are so cautious in what they say about the inner lives of animals.

Dr. McElligott returns to the subject of worrying goats.

"OK, then, while goats don't worry, they will certainly have concerns, and these concerns will be based on how they've evolved. In the wild, an animal like a goat is a prey animal. They have to eat and go to the water hole to drink and so on, but they have to balance these needs with the risks inherent in trying to satisfy them. So at the same time as eating or whatever, they're being vigilant for predators, always being slightly on edge."

So my concerns as a wild goat would be how to eat food and how to avoid becoming food. I've never been a prey animal. Constantly being on edge because of the risk of suddenly being pounced on and eaten alive does sound a bit stressful, but hey, I live in gentrified urban Bankside, where I could get run over by a bus or a millionaire businessman in his sports car at any turn. Every animal has to live with the risk of sudden death, but only humans suffer from being able to consciously worry about it, especially with regard to all our lovers, friends, and family. However, being herd animals, goats do have social concerns as well.

Dr. McElligott goes on to describe the social lives of goats. In the wild they generally hang out in sex-segregated groups, and each group has a well-defined linear hierarchy. The dominant male or female goat gets to sleep in the best places, gets to eat whichever food it wants, and generally guides the movements of its herd. The pecking order (a term taken from the strictly hierarchical bullying in flocks of chickens) continues down through the herd. So if I, as a lowly goat, find a particularly good patch of fresh green grass or a nice, warm, dry spot to bed down in and a goat higher in the social hierarchy comes over, I better move sharpish or I'll be asking for trouble.

The strong hierarchy is a way of avoiding having to fight over every-thing all the time, as everyone knows who's their boss and knows their place. Of course, sometimes you want to test your place or, if you've just been introduced to the herd, you have to establish your place, and that results in some clashing of heads and manoeuvring to hold the high ground and establish dominance. But it's not all butt, butt, butt; a goat has friends, too, forming allegiances and hanging out much more with some individuals than others.

So as a goat, I'd have to survive in this social setting where domi-nance plays an important role: making friends and avoiding stepping out of line unless I want to cause a fracas.

Keeping track of one's place in the herd is cognitively taxing, espe-cially because goats in the wild do what ethologists call "fission-fusion": smaller splinter groups wander off from the main herd, spend some time together, and then rejoin everyone later. This means that the company a goat keeps is always changing, so not only does a goat have to remember who likes it, who it needs to avoid, who it can dominate, and who it has to submit to, it also has to make adjustments to its behaviour depending on who it's hanging out with at any particular time. For example, I might find myself the highest-ranking member of the goats I'm with and need to have the nuance to realise that now it's me who's boss. And if I'm not the dominant goat amongst my current set of companions, I'd have to work out strategies to have *some* success with food and the ladies, like noticing when my superiors' attention is elsewhere.

It's thought that the demands of living in these complex social environments is one reason why goats, humans, dogs, and many other social creatures evolved our sophisticated cognitive skills. How intelligent are goats, then?

Bob at Buttercups has some great tales of goat cleverness. Thirty-two of his goats are survivors of a series of experiments the Royal Navy conducted to find out how a human would fare when escaping from a submarine at different depths. This involved putting the goats into a hyperbaric chamber and seeing if they got the bends at different pressures (they used goats because their respiratory physiology happens to be a close analogue to ours). Bob says that the Navy's goat handlers told him that after a while they realised that some of the goats seemed to develop a limp when being led to the pressure chamber (they had to be healthy at the start of the test or they couldn't be experimented on), but on being returned to their pen, the limp would miraculously clear up.

I am somewhat incredulous when I hear this anecdote: "Really? They faked a limp to get out of being experimented on?" *Sure*, Bob. Goats understand experimental method. Goats can *fake* a limp. Yes, you really do love these goats, don't you, Bob?

Just to make sure I am not being *too* unfair to Bob, I do a Google. Bob's story immediately seems more credible in light of the fact that the world, it seems, is full of both wild and domestic animals faking it. There's even a funny video of Mr. Snuggles, a cat, faking a limp so he's allowed inside the house. Bob also tells me that they've had to fit extra locks on all the pens because a couple of the goats have learned how to slide the bolts and let themselves out. He'd been trying to get his goats to bed in their pens one night, when he realised he'd put a few of them to bed twice.

It turns out, not only were they letting themselves out so they could carry on romping around, but they'd gone around to the pens of their friends and unlocked them, too.

I ask Dr. McElligott about goat cleverness but phrase my question in a way that clearly gets his goat.[3]

"Are goats as intelligent as, say, a three-year-old child?"

"Arggggh!" Dr. McElligott is almost squirming in annoyance at my question.

"I hate those comparisons. I saw a headline: 'New Caledonian Crows Are as Clever as Seven-Year-Olds.' Hmmm, yeah…They did some cognitive testing with them and applied the same tests to children, and children have to be seven years old before they start getting the tests right. But nevertheless, you don't know what's going on: the behaviour may appear very similar, but you don't know what's going on in their brains. But really why it annoys me *so much* is because I think the animal should be interesting in its own right, not just because it can beat a seven-year-old. Because the opposite of that argument is: If an animal is not as intelligent as a seven-year-old, is that animal worth less? Should we be able to treat it badly, or at least not treat it as well as we could? Has it less value? I think, No!"[4]

As I'm getting up to leave Dr. McElligott in peace, he asks the question that I'd been fearing and purposely ignoring due to the unsavoury implications: "Hang on. I didn't ask, but I assume you're going to be a male goat? Because there are key sex differences…"

My sex as a goat and my sexuality as a goat are questions I have just not wanted to think about. I guess I thought it was implicit in my funding application that I was going to remain male when I became an elephant because I'd nowhere said, "I want to be a transgender elephant."

---

3 The phrase comes from horse racing (and I shan't apologise for using it). A goat was put in the stable with a twitchy racehorse to keep it company and calm it down. Jockeys would try and steal their rivals' goats the night before the race so their horses wouldn't be on top form the next day.

4 And, of course, the parallel argument is that if the treatment of animals depends on whether they're as clever as seven-year-old children, then humans with a mental age less than seven should be fair game for the conditions in battery farms. But then we're speciesist, according to the philosopher Peter Singer.

Transgender *and* trans-species? Well, I think that might be attempting to explore too many issues at once.

But sex is obviously a big part of animal life. From the Darwinian perspective, sex is the *whole point* of animal life (though for us individual animals, that's pretty irrelevant: no one has sex out of an obligation to their deoxyribonucleic acid, right?).

However, I'm not sure I'm ready to go "all the way" for this project. I am sure my girlfriend would be extremely upset if she were cuckolded by a goat. This having-sex-with-a-goat thought opens up a whole can of worms, the eating of which would, in my opinion, be greatly preferable to the aforementioned act, if one were forced to choose. Honestly, gentle reader, this project *has not* been some terrific ruse to justify interspecies "canoodling." Of course, from an artistic point of view, that level of commitment would add a lot. Certain of the more avant-garde galleries in Berlin would, I'm sure, be much more interested in showing that kind of work. It would also help the project reach a wide and diverse audience (a big tick as far as the Wellcome Trust is concerned), in that it would stir up an immense media furor: "Largest Biomedical Research Charity in the World Funds Designer to Have Sex with Goat." I, for one, would read an article with that headline. I'm less keen for the subject of the article to be me, however. It would be quite telling if I were to find myself on trial for one count of gross indecency, one count of bestiality, one count of misuse of charity funds, etc. In fact, that legal question and its defence gets to the heart of the project. Because if I need to stand up in court to defend my actions of having had, um, "carnal relations" with a goat, it will mean— in a way—I will have succeeded in my project beyond my wildest hopes. Because I will only have had sex with a goat if I wanted to have sex with a goat, and I will only have wanted to have sex with a goat if I have managed to adopt the mindset of a goat to the extent that I have developed the deep goat instinct to seek out and mate with other goats.

I obviously want the project to be as successful as possible, so…Oh, dear. Is that really what I'm heading for here? As a human, I don't want to have "relations" with a goat. But what if I manage to be a goat so well that I do? This is a conundrum: wanting to be a goat necessarily implies wanting to have sex with other goats; hence the success of my project would be resoundingly demonstrated if such an act were to take place. How did I get myself into such a philosophical interspecies love tangle?

Luckily, nature and Dr. McElligott present a way out. Goats live in groups strictly segregated by sex, only coming together for the rut when the female goats are brought into estrus. In fact, it's thought that it's the smell of the male goats that does it, and male goats make a great effort to direct their pee onto their own goaty beards in order to increase the force of the smell they carry and thus make themselves more attractive to the females. That means that even if I succeed in becoming goat-me to such an extent that I want to have sex with another of *my own* species, I will only be able to do so at a certain time of year. In our climate, the rut is

Pan having his wicked way with a goat. This statue was found in
the ruins of the Roman town of Herculaneum, which, like
Pompeii, was buried under metres of ash from the eruption of
Mount Vesuvius in AD 79: further evidence that humans have been
thinking about all this stuff for a very long time.

around August. So as long as I leave it until after then to take up life as a goat, I shouldn't have to get involved in lovemaking with anything/one. I want to give the rut as wide a berth as possible, but I also need to make an Alpine crossing to satisfy the conditions of my grant. The weather in the Alps is not at all friendly in the winter months, the winter beginning in earnest by October. I appear to have quite a narrow window of opportunity, bracketed by avoiding any possibility of conjugal relations with she-goats and not dying atop a mountain during a fatal change of weather.

* * *

How best to transform my mind into the mind of a goat? Well, we already must have a lot in common. I mean, if life on Earth began 3.8 billion years ago and the last common ancestor of goats and humans lived only about five million years ago, we share the vast majority of our evolutionary history. To me, this suggests that deep down there's an inner goat in all of us. Like goats, we were once wild animals. Up until just ten thousand years ago, humans wandered the landscape as hunter-gatherers, living in small tribes of about one hundred fifty individuals—herds, if you will. In terms of evolution, it's a blink of an eye since we began living in vast cities, sitting on chairs, with access to sweet and fatty foods throughout the year that we don't even have to chase in order to gorge ourselves on. Goats have accompanied us in our transition from wild hunter-gatherer. One species of goat is now domesticated, and, interestingly, a good argument can be made that we've been domesticated, too.

Nine species make up the genus *Capra* (as in Capricorn). Eight of these live wild, with ranges across North Africa, Europe, and Asia Minor, including the majestic Alpine ibex, which roams high in the European Alps (the Rocky Mountain "goat" of North America technically isn't a goat). The bezoar goat, which is still found in the mountains from Turkey to Pakistan, is the species that gradually was turned into the common domestic farm goat and has since been transported across the world by humans.

Our close relationship with goats began in about 9000 BCE in a place known as the Fertile Crescent. This area around the foothills of the

Interspecies nursing.

Zagros Mountains, where Africa meets the continent of Eurasia, is where tribes of our hunter-gatherer ancestors first stopped roaming around hunting and gathering, settled down, and took to planting and tending instead. It's the cradle of agricultural civilisation.

These earliest farmers must have decided that rather than trying to creep up on these constantly on edge and frustratingly nimble creatures so as to get close enough to kill them, they could save themselves a whole lot of bother by keeping a few captive somehow. And even better, if they kept at least one of the pesky male ones about, their stock would replenish itself just by letting nature take its course. Thus the bezoar goat was the first animal we domesticated as livestock (some enterprising wolves had become man's best friend thousands of years before). As well as goat meat, as a bonus we got the goat milk to feed to our kids and make into goat cheese to eat as adults. Processing the milk into cheese was necessary before it could be consumed by adults because processing greatly reduces the amount of lactose present; it was another few thousand years before the genetic mutation occurred that caused the digestive enzyme that breaks down the lactose in milk to persist into adulthood. The human is the only animal that doesn't stop drinking milk once it's weaned, just swapping from human mother's milk to that from alternative species. And it's only about 35 percent of humans, mostly hailing from northern Europe, that can even indulge in this odd behaviour without becoming rather ill.

As today's farmers do, the first farmers slaughtered most of the juvenile males (archaeologists have found piles of male goat bones) because only one billy goat is needed to replenish the stock and you can't make cheese from male goats. They probably kept the least troublesome males, that is, the ones that showed the least aggression and fear towards humans. And so, over the generations, these captive wild bezoar goats gradually became genetically less afraid of humans and less aggressive. For some reason, becoming tamer as a species is associated with a suite of other changes, too. Not all of these changes apply to all species, but generally horns and teeth get smaller, builds get less stocky, faces get flatter, ears tend to go floppy, and adults retain more juvenile behaviour: more play, more homosexuality, and greater tolerance of other individuals. Additionally, and in all species, domestication has been associated with a shrinking brain. Dogs have smaller brains than wolves, common goats have smaller brains than bezoar goats, and pigs have smaller brains than wild boars. And, interestingly, over the last thirty thousand years, human brains have been shrinking, too. In fact, the people responsible for carving the Lion Human of Hohlenstein-Stadel had an extra tennis ball's worth of brain compared with us. They were also stockier in their build and had larger teeth and more prominent, muzzlelike jaws.

This pattern leads to the intriguing idea that humans have also been undergoing a process of domestication, a selection to become less aggressive. Only we've domesticated ourselves. How might this process of self-domestication have happened? As related by Harvard professor of biological anthropology Richard Wrangham, it could have gone like this: if *someone* (it's pretty much going to be an angry young man) keeps disrupting the group because of his violent temper, well, the rest of the group might get together and decide enough is enough and that they need to do something about said young man. So that something happens: the rest of the group collude and bash him on the head with a handy rock or push him off a handy cliff or stick him with a handy spear. Rough justice, but problem solved.

So just as our ancestors likely selected out the most aggressive and difficult bezoar goat males for the chop, a similar selection could have been occurring over the past thirty thousand years of human society. Certainly capital punishment has been a big part of human society, probably for as long as human society has existed. One of the oldest known systems of justice, the Code of Hammurabi, which was literally written in stone nearly four thousand years ago, metes out capital punishment for all sorts of crimes. And studies of peoples who live in hunter-gatherer tribes in New Guinea today find capital punishment is the cause of death of over 15 percent of males in the group. So if the troublemakers are weeded out early, before they've had time to have many children, well, gradually, so the theory goes, the genes that tend to make someone aggressive and quick to anger don't get reproduced as much in the population.

So cold-blooded, premeditated aggression, like deciding to cooperate on getting rid of a troublemaker, is responsible for a gradually diminishing tendency in our species to jump to hot-blooded, angry, reactionary aggression, which has led to our self-domestication. And, as with other species, this caused our body builds to become less stocky, our faces to flatten, our brains to shrink, and our behaviour to remain more juvenile, so even as adults we're curious, can learn new things, and generally can be more tolerant of the behaviour of others, even in a crowded tube carriage.

Today's smaller brains *could* be caused by our self-domestication, or they could be evidence that we're just dumber as a species than we used to be. If the latter, then one theory as to why our brains are shrinking and we're dumbing down is simply because our lives are less dependent on being clever; the environmental pressures selecting for intelligence have lessened. The reasoning goes that as our societies have grown, people who wouldn't quite have had the brains to survive and have children in the past manage to scrape by on the margin of the group. We're not talking about some sort of prehistoric National Health Service, just that over time people's survival has depended less and less on their own wits.

But which theory is right? Well, considering the timescales involved, there's no direct way of knowing if we're getting dumber or if we're getting domesticated (until some enterprising/mad scientist/ evil genius has a go at creating a prehistoric human from ancient DNA). But there is some evidence that we're gettin' stupid. Reaction times correlate somewhat with intelligence. In the 1880s, Francis Galton, an early eugenics advocate working at University College London, measured reaction times of over three thousand of his fellow Victorians. Comparing these measurements to modern results shows our average reaction times are slower, to the tune of 250 milliseconds for men and 277 milliseconds for women. The scientist who made the comparison calculates that the difference corresponds to an underlying decline of 13.35 IQ points since Victorian times.

But there's also evidence from IQ tests that suggests we're getting cleverer. Any IQ test, before it's made available to be used, will have been standardised. The prospective IQ test is taken by a representative sample of the population that the test is aimed at, and then it's adjusted so that the average score that will be achieved by members of that population will be 100. Professor James Flynn, a psychologist at the University of Otago, noticed that when people today take a test that has been standardised for the population of a few years ago, their average score is greater than 100. That is, when an "average person" today takes a test from, say, 1996, they'll get a slightly better than average score on the old test. The effect is consistent across populations and works out to an average improvement of about three IQ points per decade.

Many explanations have been offered to explain this general rise in IQ, such as improved childhood nutrition, but Flynn argues that the "Flynn effect" is down to people getting more used to the kind of thinking that the tests measure. In his book *What Is Intelligence?*, he references some interviews done by a Soviet psychologist, Alexander Luria, who travelled to remote ares of Siberia early in the twentieth century to interview the people there. He asked the kinds of questions on IQ tests, for example: "All bears are white where there is always snow; in Novaya Zemlya there is always snow; what colour are the bears there?" Errrm, white, obviously. But the correct answer was not obvious to the preliterate hunting peoples Luria was talking to. For example: "I have only seen black bears, and I do not talk of what I have not seen." Even when verbally prodded towards the correct answer, his interviewees (who tended to be the chief men of the tribe, so certainly not dunces) would insistently reply

with answers like "Such a thing is not to be settled by words, but by testimony. If a wise man came to us from Novaya Zemlya and testified that
bears were white, we might believe him."

I'm not sure if Luria interviewed any Yukaghirs on his trip through
Siberia, but the sorts of responses he got demonstrate a different view
of what's important and how the world works to the view implicit in IQ
tests. Learning to read (and getting an education) doesn't just open up the
range of things we think about, but fundamentally alters how we think, in
ways that aren't necessarily obvious to us.

So thicker or more docile, or even thicker and more docile? As with
anything that concerns human intelligence, especially whether it's going
up or going down, the matter remains the subject of some debate. But
regarding the intelligence of domestic animals verses their wild counterparts, it turns out that big-brained, wild wolves are only better than their
domesticated, small-brained cousins, dogs, at solving some types of puzzles. Wolves excel at things like finding routes out of mazes and getting
food out of boxes, whereas dogs trump them on puzzles that require
understanding social cues. Perhaps something similar has happened with
us and with goats: our brains may have shrunk, but the focus of our intelligence has shifted rather than diminished.

*　*　*

Whether we are in fact both domesticated or not, goat behaviour and
human behaviour necessarily share similar roots. If we widen out to animals in general, it becomes quite difficult to pin down what separates us
from them. There is a long and unesteemed history of people pronounc-
ing that X is what separates humans from animals—tool use, agriculture,
large-scale cooperation, laughter, grief—only for an example of nonhu-
mans doing X to turn up. Ants farm aphids, bees cooperate, rats laugh
when tickled, elephants grieve. As for tool use, in the early 1960s a young
Jane Goodall was the first scientist to observe chimps in the wild stripping
the leaves off sticks and using the sticks to fish for termites. Interestingly,
Liberia's five-cent stamp from 1906 features an illustration of a chimp
fishing for termites with a twig, a reminder that just because it's not yet

A chimpanzee using a tool to fish for termites on
a Liberian stamp from 1906.

been scientifically observed doesn't mean it isn't already out there: we
don't know everything about our world, and new discoveries come along
and change what we think we know. Since the 1960s chimps have been
documented using all sorts of tools in the wild, as well as passing their
knowledge on to the younger generation and so even transmitting culture, but up until Goodall's observations, anthropologists saw toolmaking
as mankind's defining trait. Upon reading her report, her mentor Louis
Leakey responded: "Now we must redefine 'tool,' redefine 'man,' or accept
chimpanzees as humans."

It looks like we resorted to redefining man, as, despite the best
efforts of the Nonhuman Rights Project (NhRP), our nearest extant
species are still not legally defined as persons. That may change: lawyers
for the NhRP were recently granted an Order to Show Cause under the
habeas corpus statute on behalf of two chimpanzees, Hercules and Leo,
captive at Stony Brook University in New York. Habeas corpus, meaning
"you shall have the body (in court)," is an eight-hundred-year-old legal
instrument that requires those holding someone captive to bring that

person to court and present proof they have lawful grounds to keep their prisoner from their liberty. The fact that the court issued an Order to Show Cause means the university had to prove its authority to keep the chimps captive. The case was heard by Justice Barbara Jaffe in New York, and the testimony presented was based not only on scientific evidence, but included citations of test cases from the era of slavery and cases where psychiatric patients have been held against their will.

In her decision, Justice Jaffe rejected many of the arguments made by the attorney acting on behalf of Stony Brook, but found herself, "for now," bound by precedent from an earlier case, where it was decided a chimpanzee couldn't legally be a person because it could not bear the duties and responsibilities of society. The NhRP in their discussion of the ruling point out that "a vast number of humans cannot shoulder duties and responsibilities either." They also note that Justice Jaffe quoted another judge, who wrote "times can blind us to certain truths and later generations can see that laws once though necessary and proper in fact serve only to oppress." As of this writing, the NhRP have filed for an appeal.

It's not just members of our most closely related living species, the apes, that are now recognised as tool users. There's that clever dingo with his stepladder, and even octopi, it turns out, are up there with the landlubbers. They've been observed slinking along the seafloor holding up bits of seaweed to use as camouflage or rolling along inside an armoured ball made of two coconut shells. Dr. McElligott had referred to cormorants as the "feathered apes": they are forever making hooks by bending bits of wire to get at little treats cunningly put out of reach by researchers. He hadn't mentioned any incidence of *goats* making and using tools; however, he did tell me about his experiment in which goats had to pull a rope, then push a lever to get food out of a box. Most of his subjects worked it out, and he found they remembered how to do it ten months later, too.

And then there's language. Sure, other animals make exclamations of alarm or anger, but for it to be language, more complex information needs to be conveyed. Well, vervet monkeys have *different* warning calls for different predators. If one of them shouts the vervet equivalent of "Snake!"

they take to the trees, but if the shout is "Eagle!" they take cover on the ground. Bees famously communicate the direction, distance, and quality of a patch of forage by the angle, length, and vigour of their waggle dance (Karl von Frisch won a Nobel prize for decoding the language of the bees in 1973). And prairie dogs (who aren't dogs but little rodents that live in burrows in the grasslands of the United States) have recently been discovered to be among the most advanced natural users of language. Not only do they have different calls to distinguish among types of predators, but they also alter these calls to describe features of the individual predator, such as its size, speed, and colour. Professor Con Slobodchikoff, the researcher who worked this out, did so by rigging a pulley system and repeatedly floating big, coloured, abstract shapes over a prairie dog colony. The prairie dogs would make calls specific to the characteristics of the particular thing floating over their home. They were effectively saying the equivalent of "Here comes another of those big blue triangle things." Brilliant.

And on to apes. While they can't talk, because they don't have the fine vocal and breath control we have and so can't make speech sounds, they've been taught sign language in captivity. For example, there's Koko and Michael the gorillas and Kanzi and Nim the chimpanzees. Koko reportedly has a vocabulary of a thousand different signs. These range from the basics such as *food, drink, nut,* and so on to words for pretty complex ideas, such as *fake, polite,* and *obnoxious.* Claims for the things that Koko and Michael have signed are pretty extraordinary. In response to a question about his mother, Michael signed, "Squash meat gorilla, mouth tooth, cry sharp-noise loud, bad think-trouble look-face, cut/neck lip/girl, hole." It's claimed he's telling the story of his mother being killed by poachers, though more sober ethologists argue that complex meanings are merely being projected by their human handlers. In a web "live chat" with Koko, and her handler Dr. Patterson, the following exchange is pretty typical:

> Question: What are the names of your kittens?
> Koko: Foot.
> Dr. Patterson: Foot isn't the name of your kitty!

Question: Koko, what's the name of your cat?
Koko: No.
Question: Do you like to chat with other people?
Koko: Fine nipple.
Dr. Patterson: Nipple rhymes with people. She doesn't sign people per se, she was trying to do a "sounds like…"

In spite of some ability by our animal brethren, our achievements in matters of telling each other stuff, combining ideas to generate new ones, and imagining stories of the past, present, and future so far outstrip theirs as to be in a different league. I happen to be writing this on the day that the European Space Agency is live blogging to the world its attempt to land a robotic probe called Philae, which has been travelling around the solar system for ten years on a robotic mothership called Rosetta (named after the engraved stone used to decipher the hieroglyphics of ancient Egyptian cultures), on a comet called 67P/Churyumov–Gerasimenko, in order to find out whether comets likely seeded the amino acid molecules from which life on Earth sprang 3.8 billion years ago. As evidence of humans' ability to have complex ideas and communicate them, the above sentence will do. Good for us![5] So what is it that makes my mind different from a goat's mind? Why can't goats think about fighting wars or going into space? What is the X that separates us from the other animals? Thomas Suddendorf, in his brilliant book *The Gap*, proposes it's "nested scenario building" and our "urge to connect." (OK, that's two X's.) In other words, it's our ability to imagine complex things and our tendency to yap about it.

To illustrate: imagine a battle of wits where my adversary has put poison in either his goblet of wine or my own, and I have to choose which goblet to drink from. I could reason about my adversary's actions thusly: "Now, a clever man would put the poison into his own goblet because he would know that only a great fool would reach for what he was given. I

---

5 Yesterday, however, was the centenary of the end of the Great War, a less edifying example of our capacity for generating symbolic thoughts (like nation-states) and convincing one another to act on (and die for) them.

am not a great fool, so I can clearly not choose the wine in front of you. But you must have known I was not a great fool, you would have counted on it, so I can clearly not choose the wine in front of me…"

Clear? What this (snippet of a scene from the film *The Princess Bride*) demonstrates is how we can run a scenario in our own mind, imagine how our actions might change the scenario, what other actors might think we'll think, reflect and reason about it, then imagine what we would do differently if that or this were to happen and so on ad infinitum (the scene continues with a lengthy chain of reasoning and culminates in a fatal poisoning). Professor Suddendorf points out that "a basic capacity for simulating scenarios seems to exist in other animals…Human development of mental scenario building explodes after age two, however, while great apes' capacities do not."

A big part of this ability to imagine scenarios is our facility for "mental time travel." This phrase means being able to delve into the past and recall what did happen, and the related ability of being able to travel into the future and imagine what might happen. All animals can learn from the past, in a way. My cat has learned that when she hears a beeping noise in the morning, if she goes and meows persistently in a big thing's face it tends to get up and give her food. But ethologists think Janet the cat isn't remembering yesterday morning specifically or last week or whenever and using it to decide how she'll behave today, or that she could imagine meowing even more annoyingly tomorrow, reasoning it might cause the big thing to provide breakfast more quickly. Cats or goats won't recall a specific event and reflect on what they could have done differently. The jury's still out with regard to chimps, however.

When I was speaking about goats with Dr. Juliane Kaminski (one of Dr. McElligott's animal-behaviourist colleagues), she put it like this: "We don't know, but we think that they might be stuck in time, not able to think about the future or the past much, because they probably don't have episodic memory. So they probably make their decisions there and then all the time."

This gets to the crux of the matter for me.

It's this ability to mentally travel in time that makes us humans such good planners and schemers, but which also allows us to worry and regret. Goats feel anxious or stressed about their present, but they don't get the same feeling about "what might happen if…" or what could have been. While yes, I do spend a lot of my time bumbling along moment to moment, I also turn my mind to remembering my past and imagining the future—and even sometimes the "if only…" of alternative presents. So to have a holiday from human concerns about jobs, bank accounts, whether I've done good things or bad, I just need to escape the tyranny of mental time travel. If you can't imagine future scenarios, you can't worry about them, and if you can't remember the events of your past, you can't regret them! So I just need to switch off my sense of time.

Brilliant! And completely terrifying. There are patients who, for reasons of disease or accident, develop lesions in parts of their brain such as the medial temporal lobe. This happened to a musician named Clive Wearing when he was forty-six years old. There is a herpes virus that lies dormant in most people; when it *is* active, it usually just travels down a nerve to your face and manifests as a gross cold sore on your lip. But it can on rare occasions go the other way—up the nerve to the brain, where it can cause encephalitis, where the brain becomes inflamed and swells up inside the skull. This is what occurred in Wearing in 1985. He thought he had the flu (as did his doctor) and so took to his bed. By the time the doctor recognised what was actually wrong, the infection had damaged parts of his medial temporal lobe and destroyed his hippocampus. One effect of the resulting inflammation was that he became permanently stuck in the present moment, unable to form new memories. He can remember aspects of his life from before he was struck down, but his short-term memory is only ever a moving window of about thirty seconds. So he can ask his wife a question, but he won't remember the answer, which can lead to endlessly circular repetitions of a conversation. When asked how he is, he reports that he's just regained consciousness for the first time. He has years' worth of diaries, pages full of lines where he's written, crossed out, and rewritten things like "*NOW, just,* finally fully woken up" again and again. He can still play the piano when he's put in front of one and can read the music, the continuous moment to moment flow of which carries him through to the end of the piece. Yet he'll report he's never seen the piano in his room before.[6]

Then, of course, there is the scourge of Alzheimer's disease, which is often first noticed by its effects on the memory. Along with regret and worry you lose nearly everything else, too, when you lose your ability to project backwards and forwards in time.

* * *

What might it be like to live completely moment to moment? Or to lose the use of language? The tragic effects of lesions in the brains of people like Wearing are studied by psychologists as one way of working out which parts of the brain are involved in the various aspects of ourselves. Another technique that's used by researchers to try to understand what's going on in there is to induce temporary "virtual lesions" using a process called transcranial magnetic stimulation (TMS, for short). When I read about these virtual lesions, I get to wondering: If I could induce virtual lesions in the parts of my brain that differ between me and a goat, the parts that are responsible for imagining scenarios and using language, would I then be able to truly experience what it's like to be a goat? This is an exciting prospect.

I email one Dr. Joe Devlin, principal investigator at University College London's Neuroscience of Language Group, who works with TMS. His reply is that he has "honestly never thought about using TMS to make someone feel more like a goat." And, while keen to manage my expectations, he's willing to perform some TMS on me so I can at least experience what it's like for myself.

My girlfriend and I arrive at University College London and meet Dr. Devlin in the corridor. He's given up his lunch hour to talk me out of my notion that I can use TMS to experience the world as a goat. My girlfriend has come along in case I end up needing some help "trotting home." He shows us into the lab, a windowless room with classic-looking research

---

6 Wearing now lives in a nursing home and has reportedly gained a kind of instinctive peace with his condition.

posters on the walls. I express some disappointment that it's not at all like a sci-fi *Total Recall*–esque brain-hacking facility, without any pulsing coloured lighting or anything, and so, accommodatingly, Dr. Devlin pulls up an MRI scan of his brain on a monitor, pulls over a 3-D infrared camera, and straps a tiny tripod to his head so as to set the scene a bit. The tiny tripod lets the 3-D camera work out where his head is positioned and oriented in space and consequently where his brain is positioned and oriented in space. He gives me a special pointing tool, and as I move it over his skull, the view of his brain on the monitor changes to match. As I move the pointer from the crown of his head down around his face and accidentally stick it in his ear, I see corresponding horizontal and vertical slices through his skull and brain and eyes and so on. It's pretty fun and actually extremely sci-fi when you think about all that's involved.

Or as the good doctor puts it: "Very science-y."

Neuroscientists use this system to help position the TMS machine's electromagnets over the head, to make sure the correct part of the cortex is zapped (my word) or stimulated (Dr. Devlin's word). As any fool knows, at any moment millions of tiny electrical impulses are propagating around the brain and through the nerves of the body, giving rise to all one's thoughts and actions and *somehow* the feeling of what it's like to be those thoughts and actions.

Now, as any fool also knows, magnetic fields and electric currents interact. So with a strong enough magnetic field aimed at your head, you can induce an electrical impulse in a patch of neurones and thus interfere with the activity in an area of your brain. It's this methodology of using a whacking-great magnet to stimulate or inhibit a brain area that constitutes TMS. The big blue cables connecting the TMS machine to the electromagnetic coils are rather thick because to generate a strong enough magnetic field to penetrate the skull requires about eight thousand amps. I joke that the lights must flicker, and Devlin says that they did until they got them changed to a different circuit. This power generates a magnetic field that goes through the skull and penetrates effectively about four centimetres into the brain. He tells me it's important that the field doesn't go too deep because a lot of the structures that are deep in the brain are

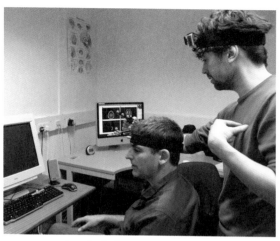

Locating Dr. Devlin's prefrontal cortex.

doing vital things like keeping your heart beating, keeping you breathing, keeping your blood-oxygen levels regulated…you know, maintaining your vital signs.

"So you don't really want to mess them up," he says.

I wholeheartedly agree.

"But we can get away with adding noise to the outer layers of the brain, the neocortex and such, because that's the bit of your brain that just does thinking and planning and language and all that kind of stuff…you know, not anything important."

He uses TMS to try and work out what the specific bits of the brain actually do and which parts they connect to. For example, by giving subjects a task to do, then giving them the same task while zapping/stimulating a brain region he suspects is involved in that task, he can confirm whether that region is actually involved by seeing whether the subjects' ability to do the task is affected. Dr. Devlin is particularly interested in language, so the tasks he gives people are things like speaking and reading, both things I'll need to be rid of if I'm to approach the world as a goat.

However, my idea of simply turning off the language bit, the planning bit, the episodic-memory bit of my brain is way off the mark. For one thing, Dr. Devlin says completely turning off a region of the brain with today's technology would basically mean killing it—creating an actual brain lesion, like a lobotomy. The virtual lesions that TMS can supply are much more subtle. They just *partially* suppress activity in a particular spot, the effects of which wouldn't be like losing a whole region or function of my brain. While the effect is subtle, it does have the advantage over lobotomy of being temporary.

I bring up the idea that goats might be stuck in time, that they probably don't have the ability to consciously recall a particular life event or to project themselves forwards into the future, whereas humans are incessantly flicking backwards and forwards: Why didn't I say that? or What'll I make for dinner?

"And the reason why I'm interested in this is because I'm thinking about how humans regret and hope."

He responds, "I suppose it could relate to language. The fact that we have the linguistic structure to talk about past events and to make them sort of items, like mental items you can work on, in some ways probably reinforces a lot of the memories. There's a lot of thinking that *you are* the stories you tell about yourself. You're with somebody for a while and their stories start to recur, or you go to a family event and everyone in the family has a slightly different story of a particular event. And the remarkable thing is that you probably remember the stories the way you tell them, not the way they originally happened. And that's how you get false memories, too. There are certain family events that everyone remembers, whether or not they were even there."

My girlfriend chimes in: "I get accused of that a lot. I get accused of remembering things before I was even born." She's come along to see me get my brain zapped.

"Right. And those stories become our memories. So I can imagine if I were a goat, I wouldn't be telling myself stories. There may be things that have happened, but I probably have a much more indistinct recollection."

If the professor could switch off my sense of language—not just my ability to speak but my sort of internal mental language, too, the blur of words and pictures that I use to mentally represent and manipulate a situation I'm remembering or imagining—then that'd be a step closer to really *being* a goat.

"Joe, could you switch off my language centre and make me lose my ability to use language?"

"No."

Arggghhh! Why is everything so bloody complicated?! (That was internal mental language.)

He continues: "In the brain, there isn't a language centre—about two-thirds of your brain, if not more, contributes to your ability to use language. There is Broca's area, which, among other things, seems to be important for people's ability to produce *speech*. So you can stimulate that and get a subject to stop speaking."

Well, perhaps that's a small step towards a goat state of mind.

"Could we try and see if we could stimulate my Broca's area? Is that possible?"

"We coooould. We'd have to go through a bunch of safety things, to make sure it would be a reasonable risk. But getting speech arrest is super hard. I can give you a feel for it, but the odds of us actually getting it in any reasonable period of time are low."

Dr. Devlin is not very positive about the chances of managing to target Broca's area without having done an MRI scan of my brain first. That is pretty much out of the question, as an MRI costs rather a lot.

"But if we do get it, it happens in two ways. One way is that it'll affect the motor area, and this sounds like the subject is having a stroke. It's sort of slightly unnerving to see."

He hurries to reassure those present in the room: "But it doesn't feel like that at all—it just feels like you're trying to speak but it's not coming out right, that there's something interfering. The other thing it does is it can get you to that tip-of-the-tongue state, you know, when you have that word and you know it begins with a *p*, but you just can't think of it."

Errm, I have that a lot anyway. He gives me a screening form. It has a list of medical conditions that I shouldn't have personally or that shouldn't run in my family, and a list of things I shouldn't have done in the last twenty-four hours, like having drunk three or more units of alcohol and so on.

As I ponder which boxes to tick, Dr. Devlin is explaining about the procedure.

"There's a nonzero but very small risk that TMS can induce seizure. So that's the hard-core risk. Medically speaking, having a seizure is not a big deal, but for normal people, particularly if you don't have seizures, it would be quite scary."

My girlfriend is listening carefully. I imagine she's asking herself what her man is doing to himself for his stupid goat obsession. "And there are some factors, like if you've had a lot of alcohol in the last day or if you've had a lot of caffeine in the last hour, that temporarily increase your risk of a seizure."

Was it one pint I had last night or three? And I did just have a coffee. Oh, well, what's the worst that could happen? A seizure! I tick no to all the questions and hand the form back to the professor, who hands me another form so I can give my informed consent for the procedure.

The TMS machine has a foot-pedal control, and when he steps on the pedal, a loud click sounds from the magnetic coil, sort of like the sound a high-voltage spark makes jumping a gap.

"The magnetic field will affect nervous tissue *and* muscle. So if I just pop it on my arm—" He puts the magnetic coil against his forearm, there's the click, and his hand sort of clenches briefly. "Do you wanna try it?"

I hold out my arm and he applies the magnetic field, and the muscles controlling my fingers clench of their own accord. I've had a few electric shocks in my time, and the effect is a bit like that: an involuntary jerk, but without so much shock. He puts the coil against the side of my head.

"Ready?"

"Mm-hmmm."

Click.

The side of my face sort of spasms, like a nervous tick, and weirdly, I feel somewhat uncomfortable inside my teeth.

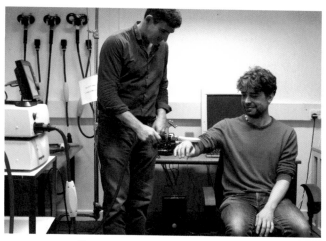

Getting the nerves in my arm interfered with.

"Yes, well, your fifth cranial nerve is there, too, so sometimes you'll get a metallic taste in your mouth as well. So that's only doing one pulse at a time. For speech arrest, we'd normally set it to do ten pulses a second for two or three seconds. So if you want to try?"

He twists the dials on the TMS machine up to *maximum power*, and the room starts shaking (not really). He demonstrates what the coil does now: tick tick tick tick tick tick tick tick tick tick tick tick tick tick tick tick, it goes when he stands on the pedal.

"Do you want to feel it on your arm first?"

"Yes, please."

He holds it over my forearm again and: "Tick tick tick tick tick tick tick tick tick tick tick tick tick tick tick tick."

My hand spasms. It looks a bit like I'm playing the piano with my right hand, the fingers moving up and down with the clicking of the TMS machine. If I were playing a piano note eight times a second, I'd be up there with the world's fastest pianists.

"Funky, isn't it? It would start to fatigue your muscle, but it doesn't do that to brain cells."

He then puts the coil to the side of my head.

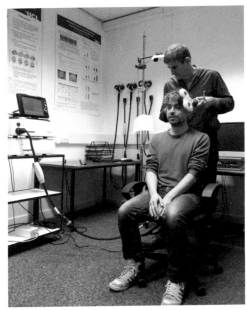

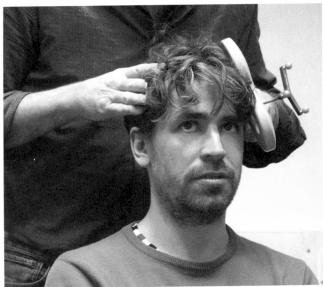

"Who's that trip-trapping over m—"

Tick tick tick tick tick tick tick tick tick tick tick tick tick tick.

My mouth sort of twitches around with the ticking and my eye muscles sort of quiver, and there's the weird pain in my teeth.

"How'd you do? Discomfort?"

"Yeah, a little bit. It sort of went down into my teeth again."

"OK. Well, the secret with speech arrest is to get you to say something overlearned, because if you just talk, you'd tend to stop anyway and we wouldn't know if it worked."

"Can I say a fairy tale?"

"Anything."

Dr. Devlin positions the TMS coil on my head, over the spot where he judges the patch of a million neurons lies that plays some role in my ability to talk. I start recounting a fairy tale I deem appropriate for the occasion.

"Who's that trip-trapping over my—" Tick tick tick tick tick tick tick tick tick tick tick tick tick tick tick tick.

"—bridge? said the troll."

"OK, so you did stop. Why?"

"I don't know."

It could have just been my natural stilted style of speech, but it could have been that the language network in my brain was being disrupted. Physically, the side of my face had spasmed, and my metal fillings felt like they were dissolving on my tongue, but mentally, I'm not sure what happened. I'd stopped saying in midsentence a phrase I knew very well.

"Could we try it again and I'll count?"

We try it again. Dr. Devlin isn't convinced he hit the spot that time, but when I review the video later, there is a slight slurry stutter as I say the numbers. Maybe that's just how I talk, with a slur, or perhaps there was some interference with my Broca's area. He recounts what happened last time he tried speech arrest without the aid of an MRI scan: he tried for forty-five minutes, and at the end the subject was really unhappy. I can empathise. After just a few bursts of TMS, the windowless fluorescent-lit experimentation room is starting to feel like somewhere I want to escape from.

Even though I promised I wouldn't, because Dr. Devlin said he "avoids research into consciousness like the plague," I decide to ask him directly about this idea of getting closer to the experience of another animal by manipulating one's brain. Is it…possible?

"It's tricky. Because at some level you'd think it should be theoretically possible, right? It's all the same tissue, serving the same function; there's nothing really fundamentally different about the biology of us and another animal. You can imagine it might be more theoretically plausible with a mammal like a goat than, say, a reptile, where there's just so much difference in the tissue and the evolutionary experience. The problem is, without being able to know what the experience of a goat or whatever is like, it's not clear how you would know whether you'd succeeded."

He has a point. It's also a point made by the philosopher Thomas Nagel in his essay "What is it like to be a bat?" We know it must be like something to be a bat (or a goat), but what exactly? Nagel claims we can never know, that it's logically impossible. Well, screw you Nagel! I'm going to try anyway.

Dr. Devlin continues: "But you could imagine that if you could start to deactivate parts of the brain, that might be a fairly crude approximation. For instance, if you could just turn off language in a person. We can't do that at the moment, but imagine you could. If you could turn it off and turn it back on, you're getting there, right? Because then you could ask your subjects, 'What was that like?' And you could give them various tests that you would think it would be hard for them to remember without a language, and when you'd turned it back on, test them to see whether they could understand them or not. But we can't do that now."

"So basically I should come back in fifty years, and then maybe you'll have the thing that can help me experience what it might be like to be a goat?"

This is what's called a leading question, the sort necessary when asking a person who's spent their entire professional career carefully avoiding wild speculation to do just that.

"I can't help but think this is probably true. Whether fifty years is enough? There's a new technique called optogenetics, which is a way of introducing a particular gene into a cell and that gene lets you turn those cells off and on with external light sources. Now obviously 'external' would be an issue at the moment, and we're not doing genetic engineering with humans. But you can *imagine* having the right frequencies so you don't have to worry about whether there's a skull in the way. Then you're getting somewhere. How you then pick just the right cells out of a bunch of ten billion, I don't know, though."

This is what I'm after: solutions! All that's needed is for me to undergo some genetic engineering to make my brain cells possible to turn off, probably with a microwave laser aimed at my head. Alas, I'm pretty sure the pesky ethics committee wouldn't like that.

"There are a lot of clever people out there trying to solve these problems—well, not all of them are trying to solve the problem of goat minds—and though I can't imagine the nature of what the solution will be, I can't help but think it's moving in the right direction. Just put the project on hold for fifty years."

* * *

Fifty years. I'd be such an old goat. If it's not possible at the moment to physically alter my perception (*without* tripping my balls off), I can at least alter my context and way of moving, like the Yukaghir shamanic hunters. I need to get rid of these roving hands with their fiddly fingers, which can't help but do ungoatlike things like holding pens and grasping door handles. I need to get rid of my hands…and replace them with hooves, so I can gallop along and leave my human troubles behind me…

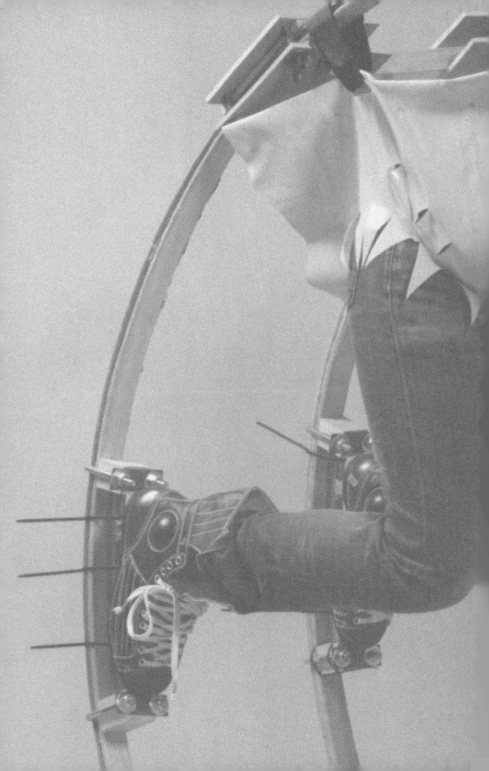

3

Body

London

(getting hotter)

The devil finds work for idle hands.

As soon as you start approaching the world without hands, you start approaching the world essentially head—and mouth—first. And that is exactly how a goat approaches the world. Dr. McElligott had told me that goats are actually very fussy eaters. When I expressed my disbelief at this because *everyone* knows that goats eat anything—it's one of the things about goats—he countered that their reputation is undeserved. Actually, what they're doing is just exploring the world with their mouth. Sure, if after exploring they find they can eat the thing, they'll eat it (who wouldn't?), but he told me that if he accidentally drops a bit of dried pasta (the goats' favourite treat) on the mucky yard floor, they won't touch it until he's gone and rinsed it for them. This fussiness, he says, probably evolved as a behaviour to avoid acquiring gut parasites (worms and such). If your mouth is your most sensitive manipulator and you're a neophilic (curious) animal, then you're going to be applying your mouth to the world a lot…giving clothes, bags, cameras, and so on a good chew, satisfying your curiosity through your primary interface with the world. What do babies do when encountering a novel object? Stick it in their mouth and give it a good gum.

The bolts on the stable door that the goats unlocked when they wanted to stay up late? They didn't unlock them just with brainpower, but in concert with their mouths and specifically their prehensile split upper lips. (A goat's upper lip is split, so it acts like two very short, highly articulated manipulators.) Our own very complicated human civilisation is the product of the tight integration of our brains with our hands. This keyboard I'm tap, tap, tapping away at (with my dexterous fingers) is a tool, after all, and making tools with our hands—and using those tools to make more tools to make more tools—is how we got to where we are today. That's the thing about brains—without some embodiment, a connection to the real world, it doesn't matter how capable your mind is (even if you are René Descartes). Where even does your hand end and your brain begin? Sure, we say our hands start at our wrists, but it's a lot less clear internally. When Joe Devlin made my fingers clench, the muscles he zapped were in my forearm. These muscles are innervated by nerves running from the spine, which in turn are connected to nerves running from the brain, which in turn are connected to networks of neurons lacing through it. Thinking in terms of systems, as opposed to external anatomy, I realise I have a brain that extends all the way into my hands. This firmly sticks me in the physical world. Imagining this network shifts my perspective on the brain as something located behind my eyes, looking out, to being present in my whole body.

A neophilic goat exploring the world.

The placing of thought purely in the brain has been called "cortical chau-vinism," emphasising just how overemphasised the brain has been in efforts to understand intelligence.

It's all very well trying to effect goat states of consciousness through mucking about with my brain, but without embodiment I'm never going to feel like a goat. Nowadays I'm firmly anti–powerful hallucinogens, and Dr. Devlin's goat-perspective brain machine won't be ready for another fifty years, so the only way I'm going to be able to achieve the shift in perspec-tive required to look at a bolt on a door and not think of using my hands to unlock it, or a bolt on a nut and not think of using my hands to unscrew it, is to not have hands in the first place. I need to turn my arms into legs and my hands into feet, aka hooves.

My first attempt at metamorphosis resulted in something that I was quite pleased with—until I actually tried to get inside it. It was basically a human-size pair of scissors, with the added feature of many protrud-ing bits of hacksaw-burred metal rod. It endangered things that humans consider nice to have: eyes, fingers, unpunctured neck, and such. Taking a step in this thing was out of the question; it was terrifying just being in it. Its numerous joints made for an overriding tendency to fold up and collapse. Thus it was exhausting just to hold myself upright, requiring all my not inconsiderable strength to avoid ending up as a crumpled heap of wood, metal, and severed digits. Galloping was out of the question.

The more joints there were, the more muscles I needed to engage to keep myself and my exoskeleton from crumpling, so for Prototype Number 2 I went to the other extreme and eliminated all joints. I focused on conservation of energy: if taking a step as a quadruped was going to be so energy intensive, I damn well wanted as much energy back from that step as possible to help with taking the next step. Prototype Number 2 was essentially two large, homemade laminated springs, like giant bows, between which I was to be suspended in a girdle. This I'd imagined would allow me to shift my weight like the pilot of a hang glider as I galloped along, my springy legs enabling me to bound over the landscape.

However, once again, getting into the thing was a somewhat terrify-ing experience. Although the total lack of joints meant that technically I

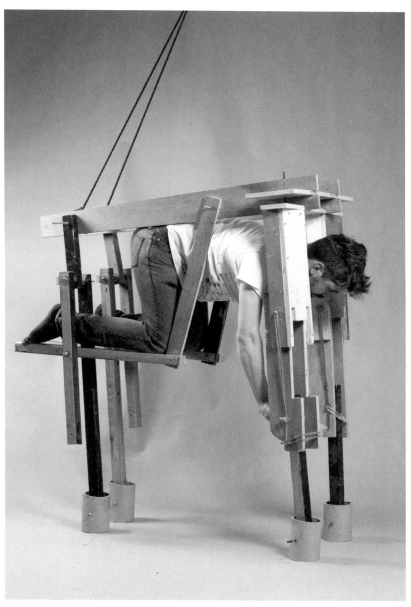

Prototype Number 1: wood, steel rod, elastic bands, cardboard tube, found objects.

could relax my muscles as the exoskeleton supported my weight, in practice my muscles remained very much clenched, because hanging facedown
from two springs that amplified the slightest shift in my weight gave me
the feeling of always being just about to topple over sideways (and again,
I'd thoughtfully included a few sharp protrusions during the making
process). While this prototype was springy in the extreme, control had
become an issue; the fact that the springy legs had no joints made it rather
difficult to move the feet, in particular to move them quickly out to the
side to prevent myself toppling over sideways. Which is exactly what happened after I managed to take one step.

Still, one small step is not to be sniffed at; indeed in some contexts
it's considered quite an achievement. I decided to remedy Prototype
Number 2's number-one defect—lack of joints—by cutting its front legs
off and sticking them back on backwards. The legs kept on dislocating
from their new ball-and-socket shoulder joints, however, so I stapled on
some ligaments made from boxer-short elastic.

I'd started to feel a bit like God, handing out legs and joints and ligaments to my creation as I saw fit. However, unlike God, I'm lacking somewhat in the omniscience department.

Nonetheless, the addition of shoulder joints to the second prototype enabled the taking of not just one but many steps. I was even able
to walk up to the end of my flat. And turn around. And walk back again.
However, this feat was not accomplished without a lot of grunting and
panting from me and squeaking and groaning from my springy wooden
body. After I'd taken possibly seventy or eighty steps, their toll was taken,
and I broke one of my back legs. Once more I found myself sprawled in a
heap of flesh and wood and bruised bone.

With these attempts in mind, I decide it's time to consult an expert.
I make an approach to God, but there's no answer, so I go to someone who
studies his designs: Professor John Hutchinson of the Royal Veterinary
College's Structure and Motion Laboratory.

After submitting to the usual pestering via email, Professor
Hutchinson kindly agrees to meet me at the campus in Hertfordshire
when he gets back from studying some "weird, weird new dinosaur

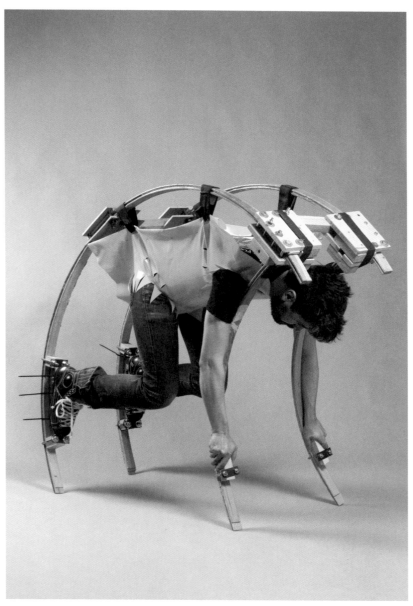

Prototype Number 2b: wood, glue, plastic sheet, steel, Velcro, elastic, cable ties, ice skates.

fossils" and "a colony of a million penguins" in Argentina. That sounds like a pretty fun work trip.

The RVC campus is "basically a farm with a bunch of animal hospitals and a biomechanics laboratory," he says when I meet him just after he's attended to the Princess Royal (the horsey one), as she unveiled (yet another) statue of a horse. Like Dr. Devlin, he's American (or Canadian, failing to judge by his accent), very busy, and an exceptionally nice guy, willing to indulge a stranger with a goat fetish.

When we're settled among the walls of books and boxes of bones of Professor Hutchinson's office, overlooked by a life-size cutout of Charles Darwin, he asks why I want to be a goat. I trot out my well-worn answer that I was upset at being a human so thought I'd become an elephant, but then was told by a shaman that I was much more of a goat, and so on and so forth.

"You started as an elephant? Ah, I would've really been your guy for elephants."

Damn! It turns out that (slightly embarrassingly) I'm consulting with perhaps the world's greatest specialist in elephant locomotion about no-longer-elephant-but-goat locomotion. But Professor Hutchinson reassures me that though his first love is elephants (along with dinosaurs), he's interested in the locomotion of other animals, too.

The starting point of our conversation is the many homologous structures in the animal kingdom, the bits of anatomy that even very different species share. So although a bird flies and a fish swims, a monkey swings, and a goat gallops, there are striking similarities in the structure and arrangement of the bones of all of their forelimbs. This was one of the lines of evidence that Darwin used to argue that animals were not put on the Earth fully formed by a designer, but rather that we all evolved from a common ancestor.

Diagrams like the one opposite illustrate Darwin's thinking, but to persons in my current state of mind, they also suggest the tantalising prospect of being able to gallop like a goat with just a few small modifications to my personal anatomy. I make my argument to Professor Hutchinson: "So with all these homologous structures between us and goats, surely it

Prof. John Hutchinson.

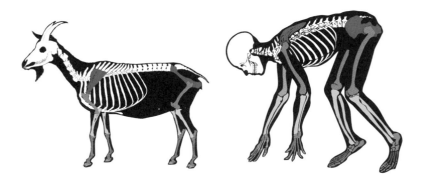

Homologous structures in the limbs of goat and man.

shouldn't be that difficult to make something that you can be comfortable galloping around in, right?"

"Ooooh." He considers his response. "Sure. But you look at a mouse, and they've got a lot of common features as well. So let's say one of the fundamental things about mice is their ability to scurry along behind skirting boards. With all these homologous structures between a man and a mouse, it shouldn't be too difficult to adjust one's anatomy so that we could scurry along behind skirting boards, right?"

Hmmm. Yes, I suppose if Annette had seen the mouse in me, it's difficult to see how I could have adapted my anatomy so I could live behind the skirting boards (in constant terror of death by Janet), even despite mice and men's similar forearm bone structure, due to this fundamental characteristic that is different: size. The professor goes on to describe the various categories of animal, moving back through humans' entire evolutionary history all the way to the amphibians and fishes.

"You see, there are common features all the way back. But there are also things that are radically different."

Ahhhh. What I think Professor Hutchinson means is that if I'm arguing that having anatomy in common with another species means we should be able to make prostheses that account for any differences and thus become like that species, well, then, why just goats? Pick any creature and I would find homologous structures on which to base my conjecture that with a bit of engineering, I could adapt myself to become that creature. The same reasoning should apply to bats, for instance: hang upside down and swoop around living off insects I catch in my mouth using only sonar? Surely I should be able to make an exoskeleton that lets me do that, since both bats and us humans have a similar arrangement of bones in our limbs, and we've both got lungs and a larynx and a mouth and ears?

So as well as all the benefits of shared anatomy from a shared evolutionary history, each species has an evolutionary history that made it unique. He tells me: "You're coming along with a lot of baggage from your evolutionary history, and you can't reconfigure that. There's so much of us that is totally hardwired and can't be changed. We've evolved so much to be bipeds, big-brained and short-armed."

"But, but, but—"

In my video of our conversation, at this point, with my conviction I can become a goat in danger of being refuted, I seem to have become quite exercised and thought it appropriate to resort to half-crawling round the office to demonstrate to the professor "just how close I am to being a goat" and how I just need to "make up for the deficiencies in my goat anatomy." Professor Hutchinson looks slightly uncomfortable at being witness to this rather bizarre display, and reviewing the recording in the cool light of another day, I am slightly embarrassed myself. But at the time it seemed liked the only way of countering his argument and keeping my dream alive.

"Hmmm," he says, considering my demonstration. Then, apropos of nothing, he exclaims, "Sure!" as though gamely deciding that if this is some kind of setup, he'll play along anyway. In any case, the grown man braying on all fours doesn't seem inclined to accept reasoned argument.

"OK, then. Well, in mechanical terms, you've got the problem that your forelimbs are shorter than your hind limbs. You need to be extending your forelimbs a bit to get your back more horizontal."

Exactly. These academics can be so slow sometimes.

"We're primates, and primates are weird. We normally put all our weight on our hind limbs, and even a gorilla puts a lot of weight back there. To be more goatlike, you've got to figure out a way to walk with more weight on your front limbs—about 60 percent of your weight on your front limbs and 40 percent on your hind legs."

I weigh 67 kilograms (148 pounds), 60 percent of which is 40 kilograms (88 pounds). That's twenty bags of sugar held up by each arm, all the time. I'm going to have to buff the hell up.

"Goats are up on their fingernails and toenails. At the front they have elongated this part," he explains, motioning to the palm of his hand, "where their metacarpals are fused."

So the joint that looks like it's where the knee should be in a goat's or a horse's back legs is actually its ankle. This leads to the common misconception that the legs of a horse "bend the wrong way." They don't, because what look like its knee joints are really its ankle joints, so it's as though it's walking around on tiptoes. (And it's not that common a misconception, because people enjoy pointing this out so much.)

"They can wiggle their toes a bit, but they're pretty stiff. A goat's got two toes that allow some side-to-side flexibility, whereas a horse has only got one, so it's even more limited."

"So they're cloven-hoofed, which means you can eat them. As the Good Book tells us: 'Among the animals, whatever divides the hoof, having cloven hooves and chewing the cud; that you may eat (Leviticus

11:3).'" (I don't directly quote the Bible to the professor, because I don't actually know the Bible by heart.)

"Yes, well. And whereas we as humans have a lot of our control spread all the way down our limbs, especially in our legs, in goats all the control and muscle in the animal is up top, with just elongated springiness down low."

"Yeah, goats do have little pinny legs."

"Exactly. And the advantage of that is it gives you a light limb, and it's easier to swing a light limb. Imagine trying to run with 5 kilogram weights. It's a lot harder to have them stuck on your feet compared to having them on your hips. So goats have everything tapered below their elbows and knees for the same reason, lengthening and lightening."

"So...could a goat run faster than a person?" I ask innocently. I know the answer, but I'm building up to broaching the subject of the gallop, and he's already a little exasperated.

"Oh, yes, definitely."

"Is that just because they've got four legs, or is it more complicated than that?"

"More complicated."

It's *always* more complicated.

"The legs are part of it, but the back plays a big role, too. When they go airborne in a gallop, they'll be flexing and then extending their back to be lengthening their strides."

"Well, my dream is to gallop."

"A gallop? Oh, boy, a gallop would be very, very hard…"

At this point, once again, I'm up out of my chair, and this time sort of manically bowing to demonstrate that I, too, have a flexible back.

"OK, yeah, that's your lumbar—the same muscles that would be powering the back of a goat—but yours are weak compared to a goat or other four-legged mammal. Besides that, a gallop would be very, very tough on your body because you've got to get airborne to do a gallop, which means the forces on your legs get higher and the stresses on your tissues get higher. Not to mention you'll just get tired out extremely quickly."

Apart from the mechanical issues, Professor Hutchinson also doubts my mental ability: "The sequence of limbs hitting the ground, the classic coconut-shell Monty Python rhythm, I think is just kind of alien to our brains."

Once again I get the distinct impression that I don't know enough to know how impossible what I'm asking is. Professor Hutchinson is trying to tell me.

"A gallop…It'd be amazing. But it's not going to happen, though. Put it this way: I think you'd find walking and trotting much more…'comfortable.'"

* * *

Professor Hutchinson takes me on a tour around the campus, which resonates with the squawks of guinea fowl. I ask why they have so many guinea fowl.

"Guinea fowl" he says, "love to run."

He takes me to the biomechanics lab, where they've built a special treadmill with a screen for doing guinea fowl virtual-reality experiments. There's another treadmill, this one tiny, for running experiments with hamsters, and a set of big cat collars being packed with sensors before being shipped to Africa, where they'll be worn around the necks of a pride of lions. He also shows me their latest gadget, an amazing x-ray video camera, which, he says, is "revolutionising the field." It lets you watch in slow motion what's happening inside an animal as it moves.

"Like in the sick bay in Star Trek," I say.

"You'd need a *very* good reason to put a human through this, though, as it takes 250 x-rays a second."

Outside, next to the lab building and tucked in an out-of-the-way corner of the yard, is a suspiciously innocuous shipping container. The professor gets a big bunch of keys with a horseshoe key ring (an actual horseshoe) and unlocks it, swinging open the heavy steel doors. Inside, the container is piled high with plastic sacks containing frozen body parts. There are sacks containing horses' heads and one containing a whole tiger; further in are some ostrich necks, loads of giraffe feet, "eleven frozen penguins, some alpacas, a leopard, a bunch of crocodiles, and lots of bits of rhinos."

Whatsinjohnsfreezer.com: Prof. Hutchinson's excellent blog. What *is* in John's freezer?

Hundreds of dead animals! (Can you spot the penguin?)

Just by the entrance are some elephant legs, bloody stumps sticking out the tops of their sacks. "We've got thirty to forty of those. Whenever an elephant dies, I tend to get sent its feet."

Sigh.

Life will have to take some fairly odd turns if I'm ever to see inside a shipping container with stranger contents. Professor Hutchinson closes up his freezer, and I follow him across the yard and into a building through some double-height doors, following the trackway of a gantry crane overhead. We emerge into a large, bright room, and in the middle, hanging upside down from the crane's hoist, suspended from a hook through one of its back legs, is a massive horse. Professor Hutchinson tells me that the hook pierces the leg at the Achilles tendon because that structure can take the whole weight of the animal. He asks me not to take any photos, though, because "it could've been someone's beloved pet."

This, then, is the dissection laboratory of the Royal Veterinary College.

Around the room are classic stainless-steel dissection tables with plugholes in the middle. On one of the tables is "the cutest little baby sheep," as I put it, embarrassing myself again, and on the next table over is a snow leopard. It's a bit less cute because it's not only dead, but at the tail end of being dissected. In fact, the only bits left that still are recognisably snow leopard are its tail and a paw.

"Can I stroke the snow leopard?" I ask.

"Sure. It might be a bit bloody, though."

I stroke the tail of a snow leopard for the first and, I'm sure, last time in my life.

"Why are you dissecting a snow leopard?" I ask.

"Well, for one, we were sent a dead snow leopard." I imagine the postman getting a snow leopard–shaped parcel out of his van. "And it'll tell us something about how the animal functions, as we're doing a study to document how the different species of cat differ: from domestic moggies all the way up to leopards, lions, and tigers." When Professor Hutchinson pushes one of the snow leopard's surprisingly large and sharp-looking claws out of its paw, it becomes very clear to me how it

Snow leopard, dissected.

functions. The snow leopard is exactly the kind of predator that would eat a mountain goat alive. Yes, if I knew I might be being stalked by a snow leopard at any time, being constantly on edge would come naturally.

"I love studying anatomy. It's got the beautiful, the macabre, the boring, the disgusting, the mundane, the shocking—it's got everything."

I'm revelling somewhat in the macabre. There is a spiky vice for clamping large bits of dead animal and a wheelbarrow containing the hooves, removed, of some creature. I ask casually how many goats Professor Hutchinson has dissected. To my surprise he says he hasn't dissected *any*.

"I've done a sheep and plenty of other cloven-hoofed animals. I did a giraffe just last week, but a goat? Can't say that I have. Almost everything but a goat, in fact. The trouble is, we just don't get a lot of them around here. No one would bring a goat to the vet school because the bills would probably be pretty high. We tend to deal with valuable animals like racehorses. Unless someone had a goat that they just really dearly loved

Winner of the "Most Beautiful Goat" title parading at the Mazayen al-Maaz competition in Riyadh.

and they were willing to spend a few hundred pounds to bring it to a top clinic, they'll say, 'Sorry, old goat, you've lived a long and happy life. It's time to go to sleep.'"

Well, I happen to know that in Saudi Arabia there are some very valuable goats. They have special goat beauty contests, and a fine-looking goat is worth tens of thousands of pounds.

"If I got a dead goat, could we dissect it?"

"Sure. I'd love to dissect a goat. It'd be interesting. But animals tend to die at inconvenient moments; you don't get a lot of notice. Frozen would be how you'd want to get it here."

Well, I would find dissecting a goat interesting, too.

Now, where might I find a beloved goat unfortunately in need of an autopsy?

* * *

Buttercups is heaven on earth for goats, but where do they go *after* goat heaven? And would it be possible to divert one from wherever they go to the dissection laboratory at the RVC, for the sake of the arts, in my case, and the sciences, in Professor Hutchinson's?

I'm a little wary of broaching the subject with Bob at the sanctuary. According to the *New York Times*, goats are the "most widely eaten" species of animal (though according to the United Nations' Food and Agriculture Organisation, which actually does surveys—counting cows from planes and so on—the *New York Times* is wrong). Whatever the case, goats are certainly one of the top ten most-slaughtered animals globally. It's estimated by the UN that a million are killed daily, for the express purpose of being cut up, so it would seem kind of inconsequential to take one goat that had already died and dissect it. Not many of those million other goats would have been given names, though.

So it is with some trepidation that I go back to Buttercups and ask Bob in a roundabout way if it might be possible to dissect one of his goats.

"No, you can't," says Bob. "We promise that when a goat comes here, it'll be looked after and respected for the rest of its life, and I think that promise continues even after its death."

So that's that. But then I explain that I'm not talking about some sort of DIY situation in my bathtub, but an expert operation at the Royal Veterinary College with a professor and his students, who get to dissect all manner of exotic creatures but never see any goats. And Bob starts to consider the idea. Buttercups doesn't have goat funerals or its own goat graveyard. No, pragmatically, any goat corpses are collected by a specialised company that takes them to Brighton to be incinerated. The rules for moving dead livestock around the country are extremely strict, due to the potential for moving around whichever possibly contagious pathogen killed the animal as well. Evidently, however, discussions among the staff and volunteers take place to which I am not party, as one of Bob's volunteer goatkeepers, who admits to "knowing all about *artists* and what they get up to," seeks me out as I wander around the yard. I assure him I'm not intending some sort of satanic goat desecration performance art. The outcome is that although some of the volunteers are unhappy with the idea, the conversation moves from flat "no" to a "maybe"—*if* I can sort out the regulatory and logistical issues.

* * *

While I await the call from Buttercups that one of their goats has answered the call of the infinite, I try to make some better goat legs with the assistance of my puppeteer friend, Ivan Thorley. Our goal is to make a new exoskeleton prototype, armed with some insight from Professor Hutchinson. The idea for the forelegs is to make hollow fibreglass "bones," into which I can insert my forearms, and aluminium tubing in lieu of elongated metacarpals, thus turning my arms and hands into legs and hooves.

Simple—yet until you've actually had to take the weight of your body—for a sustained length of time—on a bit which isn't meant to take that weight (like the flesh of your forearm), you just don't realise how much heavy baggage you carry around with you, as you. We make *some* progress; it certainly produces the best walking gait of the exoskeletons so far. However, it's difficult to optimise the structure, given the subtleties of wrist joints and weight distribution and the significant problem of how to minimise the pain where body meets machine. In the end, what our exoskeleton really excels at is cutting off the circulation and giving painful Chinese burns.

It strikes me that we are running into a lot of the same problems with our exoskeleton that, I imagine, arise for prosthetists when making a new limb for an amputee. So I refer myself to a prosthetics clinic at the University of Salford, where a Dr. Glyn Heath works. Dr. Heath is a prosthetist but got his PhD in zoology, an unusual combination that gives me hope he might have some advice on my conundrum. To my delight, he invites me up to the clinic, so off I hop to Salford, my latest front legs folded into a suitcase.

Dr. Heath, prosthetist, zoologist, and (I discover) charity worker, union rep, and self-described "pain in the neck to those in power," explains that he invited me for an initial consultation because he has become intrigued by this proposal.

"It's totally alien to the way I normally think, you see. And then it got rather interesting…I couldn't help but try and think of ways to do it. Completely wrong-footed by it."

I suppose it's fairly rare for a prosthetist to make *front* legs. But actually Dr. Heath does occasionally make prosthetics for animals, pet dogs, and such. So he's made a couple of front legs before but concedes he's never made front legs for a human. I ask if any of his patients has ever asked for a special job, a replacement limb with interesting modifications or improvements over the biological original.

"Not a chance. In all of history no one has made a prosthetic that improves on the human body."

"What about those carbon fibre ones worn at the Paralympics?"

"The people wearing them don't go about in those all day, do they? They take them off after the race. They're specialised for only one specific type of activity, you see."

"What about modifications?"

"Well, suits of armour were the first prosthetics. They might stop your head getting cut off, but they stop you doing most everything else, too, ha, haha!"

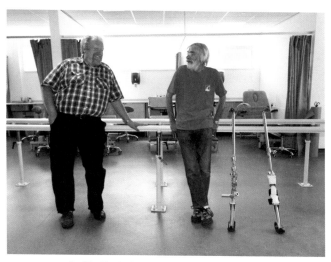

Dr. Glyn Heath, Geoff, and the legs I made with Ivan.

Dr. Heath introduces me to his prosthetics technician, Geoff, and I explain my dream: to be free to gallop like a goat. Their reaction is similar to that of Professor Hutchinson, involving a sort of expectation management. They know a lot that I don't but are seeking to let me down easily. But whereas with Professor Hutchinson the focus was on the millions of years of evolutionary distance between people and goats, with Dr. Heath and Geoff the conversation quickly turns to pain. These are clinicians, not researchers. Much of their job involves making practical interventions in an attempt to alleviate the pain caused to people by their own bodies, bodies that are malformed either from disease or from surgical intervention. And when I say I need to *cross the Alps* on four legs, there is a bit of an outcry.

"Ho, ho, ho!" Dr. Heath is a jovial fellow and punctuates his conversation with laughter. "How long have you got? Maybe if you were a carnivore…because then you could just sleep for eighteen hours a day! A ruminant has to cover a bit more ground, though, ha, haha." He continues, "I would dispute in the strongest terms whether you'd be able to walk for more than twenty- or thirty-minute stints—at an absolute maximum!

And it won't even be fatigue that'll stop you. It'll be the pressure on parts of your body that will *destroy you* before you fatigue."

Geoff chimes in: "It'll make you ache in places you didn't know you had."

"Yes, Geoff's right. We can *reduce* the pain by making things more comfortable, but the pressure on parts of your body is still there, and the pressure will destroy you."

Destroy is a strong word, but they are emphatic. What about the man who had a prosthetic leg and did a marathon?

"Well, that's good for him," says Geoff, "but from a clinical point of view, I think that's madness. I'd like to see his stump afterwards; it'd be like a tenderised ham. But even then, at least he's still upright; you're gonna have a whole host of other problems. Like how are you gonna hold your head up? That's gonna bloody hurt 'n' all. Goats and what have you have something called a nuchal ligament. It runs along the back of the neck, like a taut piece of rope, and helps them keep their heads up. But you don't have one of those. And I'll tell you what: I'd say you're better off not making one, because it might make you *too comfortable*. We want you to get tired, see, so you have to stop. We don't want you to keep your head up for too long, as it could affect your nerves, as well as the blood flow to your head."

"Ha, ha. I think the blood flow to his head might've been affected already, Geoff!"

"You really want to be safe, particularly where your neck and spine are concerned, 'cos otherwise you'll be back here as a patient."

"Yes, actually, Geoff's right," Dr. Heath says, becoming serious. "We don't want you back as a paraplegic."

I have to agree. The goal is to gain, not lose, the use of some legs.

I ask what the most common reason is for needing a prosthetic limb. Dr. Heath has just returned from Turkey, where he was working with a charity, training prosthetists. There the most common reason for a prosthetic is the trauma of the war next door in Syria. But in societies where civilians aren't subject to mass violence, to my surprise, most amputations aren't due to gruesome accidents with power tools or traumatic events like road accidents, but poor lifestyle "choices" (bad diet and smoking). These cause diabetes, which can cause damage to the nerves in the limbs, which means pain messages from the limbs aren't transmitted properly. So someone can develop a small foot problem, say, a blister, and just ignore it because it's not registering as painful, so it's easy to ignore. And the person will just carry on walking on it, ignoring the problem—because, after all, sometimes it can be a hassle and in some places expensive to see a doctor—and the little blister develops into a sore, still painless, which gets worse and worse until it becomes gangrenous. And by then it can have gotten so bad that the only remedy is to amputate the limb. There's a good evolutionary explanation for why pain is painful: it's difficult to ignore. So Geoff's idea that they *want* me to feel pain as a goat seems less gratuitous and more like a sensible precaution.

Unhealthy lifestyle being the number-one cause of amputations strikes me as a peculiarly counterclockwise chain of cause and effect. Human beings are supposed to be good at modifying our environment. After all, we modified wild species of grasses into domestic wheat and rice and corn, and have modified 37 percent of the Earth's land area to grow these food crops and raise billions of livestock animals. But now the environment we've created, rich in sugar and fat and alcohol and tobacco, with the majority of work and entertainment involving sitting in a chair, seems to be modifying us back.

I reassure Dr. Heath and Geoff that this becoming-a-goat-and-crossing-the-Alps business is entirely my own responsibility, that I'm an adult of sound mind and judgement and that if I did end up back at their clinic as a patient, it would be entirely my own fault and so on.

"OK, we'll make you some legs," Dr. Heath says.

Result.

"But it'll take a while. How long have you got?"

I explain that I'm keen to avoid the rutting season but also keen to not freeze to death, so "until late September." They've both got prosthetics to make for people not interested in holidaying from humanity, meaning they'd be working on mine outside normal clinic hours, so Dr. Heath would like to get going as soon as possible. He asks to see my quadruped

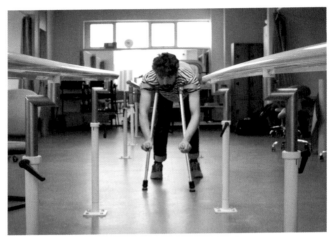

Practising walking as a quadruped round the prosthetics clinic.

gait. I get out my pair of sawn-off crutches that I've made specially and set off round the clinic. I'm pretty slow at first, but I gradually achieve a four-legged walking gait quite well.

He and Geoff are commenting as I do so, criticising everything that's wrong with my two-legged body's attempt at becoming four legged.

"Your back legs are too long. Your pelvis is about 135 degrees out of alignment. You need at least 60 percent of your weight on your front. You're plantigrade, not unguligrade, but we could probably make you an AFO that would give you digitigrade rear-foot action." (An AFO is an ankle-foot orthosis, I later learn.)

I'm keen to graduate from walking, so I clamber up on a chair, intending to jump off again, goatlike, front first. However, that deep instinct for preserving the integrity of one's body kicks in, and I'm suddenly a bit timid.

"You do that sort of thing and you'll dislocate your shoulder, break your clavicle, and knacker your ligaments, and that's no fun," Geoff says. "The reason why a goat can jump from such great heights is its body can fall away from its scapula. It's got no bony connection between its front limbs and the rest of the body. So when it lands on its front feet from a great height, its body just carries on and springs back, like the body's joined to the top of the legs with elastic bands. You, however, have a bony connection between your arms and the rest of you—at the clavicle."

There are, of course, many other subtleties in the human body that you just don't think about when you're healthily moving around in daily life, but which become apparent when they stop working so well (or when they start getting in the way of your desire to gallop). Joints like knees and elbows, I thought, had a fairly obvious range of motion, but in fact they are moving and adjusting in all sorts of ways. As for the shoulder, "it's all over the place."

"You take your movement for granted, but when you actually try and work out what's going on with just a single joint when you walk around, well—"

This means that Dr. Heath and Geoff want my goat suit to have as few prosthetic joints as possible, because their external joints won't be

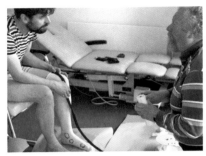

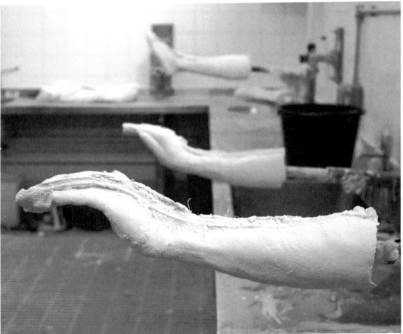

Dr. Heath making plaster casts of my limbs.

able to match the range of movement of my biological ones, so will in fact restrict my movement: the more there are, the more encumbered I become. My vision is scaling back from a sort of full-body exoskeleton to something a little…simpler.

Geoff brings out a dusty box of prosthetic joints, which he calls "the art deco of the prosthetics world." They have a lot of them gathering dust in the stores, because they're for a style of prostheses once very common, "just after the war." He's not talking about the latest Middle Eastern war, either. Basically, they're the type of joints used for making wooden legs.

"You get the odd old boy who still wants them," he says, and he reckons they're also almost perfect for human-goat prosthetic legs. Simple, strong, able to withstand the toughest Alpine conditions.

"How fast do you think I'll be able to gallop, then?" I ask hopefully.

"I don't think you'll ever be able to gallop—"

"No, you'll never gallop," Dr. Heath confirms. Cue sorrowful violins.

However, as I get back to pacing around as a quadruped with my sawn-off crutches, to Dr. Heath's absolute amazement I'm able to break into a trot. It's difficult physically, but mentally, coordinating my four legs in a trotting pattern seems to come naturally. Dr. Heath wonders out loud if there is some residual feedback in my body from when we diverged from quadrupeds. If he were a younger man, he says, he'd want to write a paper on me!

Later he gets me to demonstrate "my trot" to the other clinical staff. I feel quite proud.

*   *   *

I'm back at Dr. Heath's clinic a couple more times in the next few days so he can take plaster casts of my limbs. He warns me:

"You'll only ever be a human in a goat walking position, constrained by your own natural anatomy. While Geoff and I make these, I think you need to do some stretching exercises to try and get more range in the pelvis and stretch your hamstrings and get your knees towards your chest."

And that is when I decide to take up yoga.

*   *   *

Poor old Venus: on her last legs.

And then I get the call. "Buttercups...A goat called Venus... Very poorly...Calling in the vet...Have you worked out the transport to the RVC?"

I have worked out transport, in that I've become a licensed haulier of Category 2 animal by-products. Yes, gentle reader, if you need some dead animals moving around Britain, I'm your man. Though I can't take any spinal cords or brains that've already been cut out of an animal, as those are Category 1.

So I drive up to Buttercups. When I arrive, Venus is still alive but very thin. Gower, the general manager, explains that the vet suspects Venus is wasting away due to something called Johne's disease. This is caused by a particularly unfriendly bacteria that moves into the gastro-intestinal tract and causes the intestinal wall to thicken, which fatally degrades the animal's ability to absorb nutrients. It's the same bacteria—*Mycobacterium avium ss. paratuberculosis,* or MAP for short—that some suspect is the cause of Crohn's disease in humans. Johne's disease is highly infectious among livestock, with the ability to quickly spread through a herd via the poo-grass-mouth vector, which is worrying Gower, so he's

Left: Well, the end comes to us all, and then that's (probably) it.
Right: Luckily she just squeezes into the fridge.

keen to verify the vet's hypothesis. This would require microscopically examining a sample of Venus's intestinal wall at autopsy, and that's what the scientists and vets at the RVC are exceptionally good at doing.

Venus perks up a bit while I'm there, but Gower says animals can often seem better for a while just before a terminal decline, and so it goes with Venus. Two days later, on Sunday, I get the call again. Gower says the vet has euthanised her, as they didn't want her to suffer unnecessarily.

So I borrow my dad's car and drive back to Buttercups to collect Venus's body.

Rigor mortis has set in, but Venus has died in quite a compact posture, so we are able to seal her in the plastic bags I've brought along. The fact that it's Sunday, however, means I can't take her to the RVC until the morning, so necessity demands that Venus must overnight packed in ice in a makeshift morgue, i.e., my fridge. (Sensitive readers, look away now.)

The following day I drive Venus's body to Professor Hutchinson's freezer. Later that evening I drive my girlfriend's sister to the hospital as she goes through the advanced stages of labour. She doesn't decide to name her baby Venus, but in anticipation of when you're old enough to read, let me take this opportunity to say: "Hello, Florence!" Though I don't mention it to your mother at the time, having had poor, dead Venus just a few hours previously in the same spot where your mother is very nearly having you does make me contemplate how both ends of the circle of life came so close to meeting in the backseat of Dad's thirdhand Mercedes.

*   *   *

Dissecting Venus turns into a two-day process, because when we unwrap her, she still needs some thawing out towards her middle. Professor Hutchinson begins by removing the skin, and after a bit of scalpel safety training, I'm allowed to muck in and help. We reveal a patch of green-blue flesh in Venus's haunch. This is where the injection that killed her was administered, dyed green-blue as a safety mechanism. If you're ever served a green-blue steak, you're probably dining on racehorse. It would be an interesting meal for other reasons, too, as the injection is a cocktail of ketamine and barbiturates.

As the dissection progresses Venus changes from the familiar form of a goat (though dead) to something unfamiliar, an interconnected system of internal organs in a cradle of muscle and bone, then back to something familiar: separate organs and bits of limb that we recognise from butchers' shops or supermarket chiller cabinets.

Now, I'm actually quite a squeamish person, so I'd been expecting to find cutting into poor old Venus quite difficult to handle. Later I will barely be able to watch some of the video that my friend Simon shoots (especially the bit where we're cutting away the skin around Venus's mouth to reveal the muscles that give her those prehensile lips), but in the actual moment it's fine—though completely weird and out of my everyday experience. For the biologists in the room, of course, it's completely routine: at the same time we are dissecting Venus, another group is dissecting an alpaca; at one stage, it seems it might've died of tuberculosis (luckily that turns out not to be the case or everyone present would've had to be quarantined). Another group is performing an autopsy on a huge, white, fluffy, dead Pyrenean mountain dog.

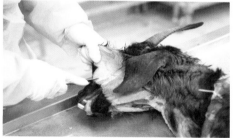

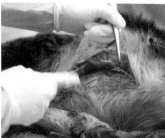

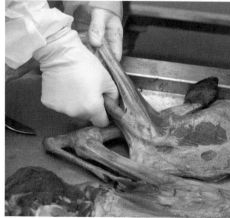

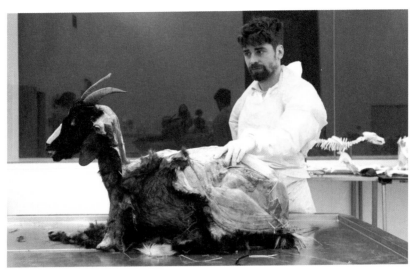

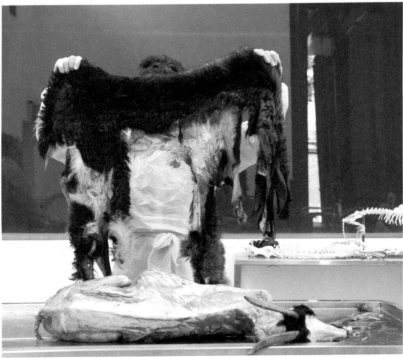

I do struggle a bit when the technician hacksaws open Venus's skull (the sound of saw on bone is somewhat emotive). And though by the end of the second day, I've really had enough of the smell of goat mingled with intestinal contents, the iron scent of blood, and the antiseptic of the dissection room, the gore of it all has been subsumed by this fascinating opportunity to explore goat anatomy from the outside in. It has hammered home just how mechanically subtle a body is: each bone in Venus's body seems shaped to optimise for multiple criteria, and connected with muscle and sinew to make a range of movements as energetically economical as possible.

In terms of engineering, designing a system that lets me adapt my existing anatomy to approach the sophistication of Venus's is finally starting to seem, um, bloody impossible.

Professor Hutchinson asks if I've seen the running quadruped robots built by Boston Dynamics with funding from the Defense Advanced Research Projects Agency. Yep, they're pretty scary.

To make a hand into a hoof, elongate the bones of the hand and fuse the fingers.

"Well, with trying to design a robot that runs around on four legs, we're *just* getting there, but it took over a hundred years of robotics research. And that's designed from scratch. Working from your existing body, with all its existing parameters, is going to be much more difficult to do."

When Professor Hutchinson has to rush off to discover new dinosaurs / attend a faculty meeting, he leaves me to assist one of his PhD candidates, Sophie Regnault, and the resident vet, Dr. Alexander Stoll. Sophie is collecting kneecaps. She's keen to take Venus's for her doctoral thesis because she has kneecaps from all manner of exotic species but none from the lowly old *Capra hircus*.

We cut off Venus's legs (and Sophie cuts out her kneecaps), and I see that, as Geoff had pointed out, Venus's thorax was basically just suspended between her two front legs in a sort of muscular sling without any bony joints, a very useful adaptation if you do a lot of jumping down off ledges headfirst. As Dr. Stoll says, "an impact like that would tear out our collarbones. Goats have no collarbones because they would just get in the way. Goats need to run, not carry shopping bags."

Nonetheless, as we work away, I can see that in gross biological terms, Venus and I—and indeed all us mammals and most of the other

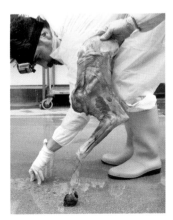

Comparative anatomy.

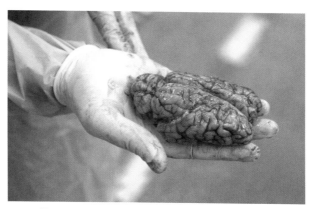

The organ that made Venus Venus. About a tenth the weight of
the one that makes us us.

animals on Earth, too—match the basic description of a fleshy tube with
openings at both ends. And hanging off our tubes are various weird and
wonderful appendages for such things as moving our tube around so it
can get more food into the intake end in order to live long enough to
make more fleshy tubes. Not the most sublime description of the animal kingdom, but true nonetheless of goldfish, finches, octopuses, spi-
ders, penis worms, diplodocuses, me, your mother, my mother, elephants,
goats, and most of the rest of us categorised as symmetrical animals. We
are the *Bilateria*, the group in the tree of life to which 99 percent of animals belong, the vast majority of which share the distinction of having a
mouth and an anus. Not flatworms, though; they have only one dual-use
opening.

So we have the same basic plan, all those homologous structures and
such, but, as I'd been learning, the devil is very much in the details. While
goats and humans are the same in many ways, since our lines diverged
five million years ago, we've been evolving into bipedal, digitigrade,
shopping-carrying omnivores, while they've specialised into quadrupedal,
cloven-hoofed, unguligrade, cursorial ruminants. We have more brains,
but what goats lack in brains, they make up for in…

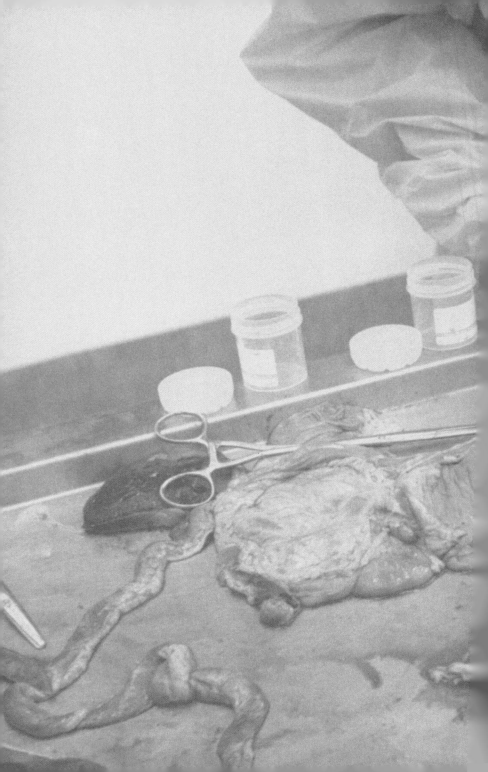

4

Guts

Goats have a lot of them.

There are many ways to skin a cat and many ways to dissect a goat. The way Dr. Stoll has chosen elegantly illustrates my feeling that we're all just tubes with appendages. With just a couple of incisions and a ta-da flourish, he's separated Venus's organs all the way from tongue to anus. He slides out the guts (and there *are* a lot of them), and we lift the whole interconnected mass over to another table.

Sophie kindly offers me some Vicks VapoRub to dab on my chin to try and mask the smell as we start to examine the gastrointestinal tract. I'm particularly interested in this part of Venus's anatomy because, as we know, one of the things that goats excel at, along with galloping and clambering around mountains, is eating. And while Dr. McElligott corrected my notion that they'll eat anything, they are able to eat a wide variety of plants, such as those that grow on the green Alpine slopes. This is an ability I very much wish to acquire myself.

Dr. Stoll traces the path these foodstuffs took through Venus as they were converted into Venus. So we start at the tongue and trace down the esophagus, past Venus's larynx, and into the bits that were contained within her abdominal cavity.

Goats are foregut digesters and confusingly also have four guts. They need all these extra guts because, like all mammals, they lack the ability to produce the enzymes that let them digest cellulose and lignin.

Goat gut microbe farm.

This seems rather an oversight, as most of the plant matter they eat is made of cellulose and lignin.

Many microorganisms, on the other hand, can synthesise these enzymes. So goats and other foregut digesters have evolved a symbiotic relationship with these microbes: they provide microbes living space in their guts, and the microbes deal with all that tough cellulose and lignin through microbial fermentation. This is a slow process, however, requiring time and space in order to occur, hence the four guts we're looking at on the dissection table.

The first two of these are the rumen and reticulum. The reticulum is a kind of small, dead-end pouch at the top of the rumen, in which ruminants store the bit of foliage they're currently ruminating on before they regurgitate it back up the throat to continue chewing it. The fact that it's

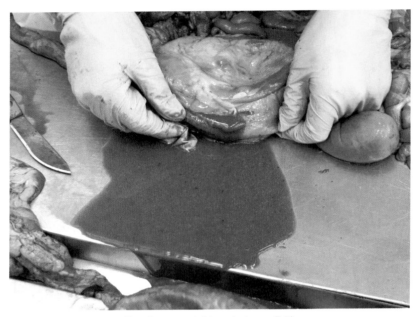

Venus's rumen and all-important rumen fluid.

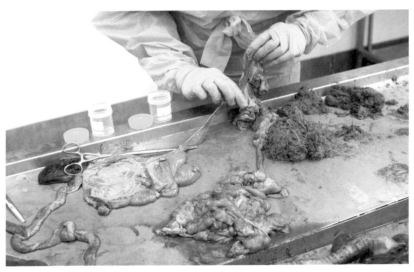

Attempting to untangle the intestines.

already been down once means the microbes have had a go at it for a while and softened it up, so it can be chewed up further before heading back down to the rumen so the microbes can really get at it again.

"So is the reticulum the equivalent of our appendix?" I ask.

"No," Dr. Stoll replies.

Sophie cuts the rumen open, and a kind of brown soup flows out, along with little flecks of Venus's last meal (looks like she went for grass). This is the rumen fluid, which is full of the microbes—the bacteria, fungi, and protozoa—that together let ruminants do what we can't: digest the cellulose in plant matter.

"The rumen and reticulum act as a big internal fermentation chamber; the bacteria that live in there do all the work," Dr. Stoll explains. "It's the bacteria in the rumen that make enzymes that actually break the grass down into what are called volatile fatty acids, because the cellulose in the grass is actually indigestible by mammals."

"So what's after the rumen?"

"Next is the omasum, which has leaves like a book and is like a physical sieve, only letting small particles through to the abomasum. It's the abomasum that is the equivalent of our stomach. Everything before is like the top of our stomachs, but gone mad. The abomasum has all the familiar acid in it and does the digestion proper."

All of these workings are wrapped in a big piece of fatty tissue called the omentum, which, according to Dr. Stoll, makes a delicious type of Greek sausage.

For us, lacking a rumen and its inhabitants, cellulose is dietary fibre. And, though important for one's bowel movements, it passes through our guts without providing much in the way of energy, whereas for ruminants it's their main source of nutrition. It's like goats have a sort of internal farm, where they cultivate the microbes in their rumen by supplying them with plenty of grass so they can grow and multiply and produce these nutritious volatile fatty acids. These are filtered into the abomasum, along with a good proportion of the microbes themselves, where the goat finally digests its harvest with stomach acid in familiar fashion. Goat eats grass, microbes digest grass, goat digests microbes.

The biopsies from Venus's intestinal tract.

The tour of Venus's gastrointestinal tract continues to her intestines. Sophie offers me a top-up of Vicks before she begins cutting them open with scissors. The contents of Venus's intestines aren't fluid like that of the rumen. By now they are much more solid, much more recognisable.

Dr. Stoll cuts two little chunks from Venus's intestinal wall to examine later under the microscope for the deadly Johne's disease–causing MAP bacteria. And that's that.

When Venus was brought into the dissection room, she was categorised as a potential biohazard, so her remains can leave only as smoke and ash from the furnace. But as we're clearing up, the lab technician offers to process the bones using their special bone-cleaning system, which would mean I could collect them and take them away a couple of weeks later. I consider momentarily: Will Buttercups be OK with me reassembling Venus's *bones*? A skeleton is surely a less emotive thing than a recognisable individual? Oh, dear, I hope I'm not about to confirm their worst fears about the arts.

I reply: "Yes, that'd be great, if not too much trouble."

"No, no trouble. *You* might have trouble putting the skeleton back together, though…"

*   *   *

The thing is, I'm not going to be very free of human concerns if every few hours I have to worry about where the next Swiss fondue restaurant

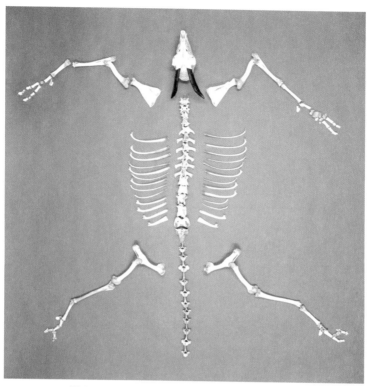

Working out which bones connect to which bones is tricky…

is (and the consequent concern of how to pay for said fondue). So I need to find a way to be able to eat grass. And not just eat grass, but digest it. Anyone can eat grass. Tragically, during the Irish Potato Famine of the 1840s, people who had died of starvation were often found with their mouths stained green from all the grass they'd been eating to no avail, because we humans lack that crucial set of gut microbes that can digest cellulose.

We do, of course, have our own set of gut microbes, our microbiome, that live in our intestines and help with our digestion. My first idea for giving myself the ability to digest cellulose was to add microbes from a goat's gastrointestinal tract to my own, using a technique called faecal

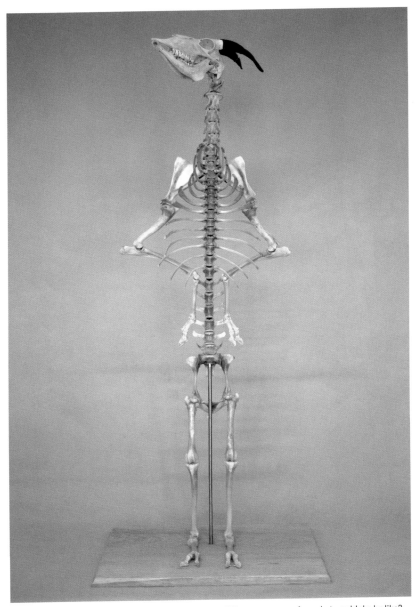

I decide to make a virtue of my ignorance and imagine: If Venus were one of us, what would she be like?

microbiota transplantation. This is a procedure usually used to replace a patient's malfunctioning gut microbiome with that of a healthy person. So I thought if I transplanted the microbes from a goat's guts into my own guts, I'd get the goat's ability to digest cellulose.

If only it were as simple as a goat-poo enema.

From dissecting Venus I now understand that in a goat, cellulose is broken down into digestible products *before* it gets to the stomach and intestines, the place where humans' gut flora reside. What I need, of course, is to make myself an artificial rumen. At this point I've been round the block a few times, so I know an artificial rumen isn't likely to be possible. But my research leads me to the Herbivore Gut Ecosystems lab at Aberystwyth University, where they use just such a device!

I give them a call and speak to the lab's leader, Dr. Alison Kingston-Smith. Her group is trying to understand what goes on in a ruminant's rumen, and her specific project is an investigation of how the plant cells themselves react to suddenly finding themselves being eaten and digested. This may seem rather niche, but the fermentation process that plant matter undergoes in ruminants like goats and cows produces methane, a potent greenhouse gas. The burps of farmed ruminant livestock together are the largest global source of methane, and emissions from livestock in general account for around 18 percent of greenhouse gas emissions, slightly more than all of the world's road vehicles, ships, planes, and trains. Understanding what's going on as plants are digested in the rumen could allow the grass to be changed or the balance of rumen microbes adjusted so as to reduce, or completely eliminate, the methane produced. That's to say nothing of simply making the rumen more efficient at turning grass and so on into animal. Considering that the global demand for meat is projected to triple by 2050, even small changes to rumen emissions and efficiency have huge environmental implications. I think I'll become a weekday vegetarian.

After explaining the broad theoretical basis of *my* project, in turn, I get specific with Dr. Kingston-Smith.

"What I was thinking was I could get a sample of a goat's rumen fluid…"

"Yes."

"And put it in a fermenter, like a big kind of bag…"

"Yes."

"And add some grass and foliage…"

"Yes."

"And then culture the rumen fluid microbes…"

"Yes. That's pretty much what we do." Dr. Kingston-Smith says. She's sounding quite jolly.

"Great! On the right track then! So then the microbes would grow, fermenting the grass…"

"Yep."

"And I could then strap this bag to my torso and spit chewed up grass into one opening and suck the cultured microbes and volatile fatty acids out another opening like a milkshake, so I can digest them in my true stomach and live off grass in the Alps like a goat."

Dr. Kingston-Smith adopts a sudden change of tone.

"No. No, I wouldn't do that if I were you."

It had all been going so well. She continues, sounding somewhat grave.

"There are…issues of safety associated with that proposal. With new sequencing technologies, we're discovering all sorts of things that are part of the rumen mixture that we wouldn't expect to be there. And some of them aren't altogether benign. The ruminant has evolved this complex mixture of bacteria, fungi, protozoa, archaea, lots of different categories of microbes. We don't know the totality of what's in there."

"Right. I see."

"There are hundreds—hundreds and hundreds—of different species in there. In the last ten to fifteen years, people have been using molecular tools to actually go in and find out how diverse the population structure is, and we're seeing that things are more complicated than we'd ever predicted."

"Right." Typical.

"And so there are still an awful lot of unknowns in there."

"Yeah…"

"Yes, so I had a feeling that's where you were going, but from a safety point of view I would *strongly* suggest you didn't do that."

Now, in general I consider myself to have a fairly robust composition, and I'm not one to shy away from the odd calculated risk, so imbibing a bit of fluid cultured from a goat's rumen wouldn't usually be the sort of thing that would concern me. I mean, the acid in *our* stomach is there to attack and break down cells, whether they be animal, vegetable, or bacterial. So I'd assume that the acid in my stomach would just digest whatever bacteria and so on I happened to be cultivating in my proposed artificial rumen. Indeed, the whole point of a rumen is to provide a perfect environment in which to grow bacteria as they feed on grass, so one's stomach can then digest the bacteria and their products in turn.

But the thing is, in researching my first nonplan of giving myself a DIY goat-poo enema, I'd, of course, read plenty of stories from people suffering from debilitating and extremely unpleasant gut conditions through being colonised by some unfriendly bacteria or other, which they were trying to cure through faecal microbiota transplants. And sure, while humans delight in eating all sorts of weird and wonderful products of microbial fermentation—yogurt, sauerkraut, kimchi, ten-thousand-year-old eggs, not to mention alcohol—and our stomach acid will usually just take care of the microbes responsible, it can also be overwhelmed (as I'd recently discovered by reheating a rice-and-shellfish dish after it'd been in the fridge for few days). So I could see Dr. Kingston-Smith's point: culturing a vat of thousands of unknown species of microbe and then eating whatever resulted on purpose could be playing a bit fast and loose with one's long-term health. The risk would be not just giving myself a bad case of food poisoning, but acquiring a permanent, debilitating gut condition as well. Turning up to my doctor's with persistent bouts of diarrhoea and describing my history would be pretty embarrassing.

After all, it was likely some sort of gut infection that did it for poor old Venus. Dr. Stoll microscopically examined the biopsies he'd taken from her intestines and saw her intestinal walls were thickened, which is consistent with Johne's disease, but didn't see any of the MAP bacteria that causes it. His conclusion was inconclusive: it *could've* been Johne's disease, or Venus could've been dying of some other unknown intestinal colonisation. I, of course, would have tried to take my sample of rumen fluid from a goat without a visible case of infection by the bacteria some scientists suspect of causing the painful and currently incurable Crohn's disease. But even then, introducing a whole range of tough, new goat-specialised bacteria into my own delicately balanced internal microbiome…Well, the results, as Dr. Kingston-Smith put it, might not be altogether benign.

* * *

The reason certain microbes can feed off grass is because they produce certain enzymes—cellulases—that break down the tough cellulose molecules into digestible sugars. This ability isn't useful to just goats. Cellulose is the main component of plant cell walls, the most abundant carbohydrate in nature. There's a big push to make biofuel from it: to ferment straw, corn husks, wood—any sort of fibrous agricultural waste—into sugars and then into alcohol. One of the ways this is done experimentally is to mix the plant waste with purified cellulase extracted from a bacteria that seems to produce a lot of it, *Trichoderma reesei* (the bacteria was first brought to the attention of scientists by the US Army, as it kept digesting the canvas of their tents on the Solomon Islands in World War II). Biofuel converted enzymatically from cellulose is a great hope of the industry. If they can break down agricultural waste into sugar and ferment it into alcohol for fuel, well, we've got fuel from waste. At the moment, however, the enzymes are just too expensive to make it economical.

Cellulase enzyme extracted from bacteria is also used in the food industry. It's mixed with the fibrous pulp of fruits left over after they've had the juice squeezed out of them to break down those fibres into sugar and convert every last possible bit of fruit into lovely, enzymatically liquefied juice. If it's used in the food industry, it must be safe for human consumption, right?! So I could use this same purified cellulase enzyme in my artificial rumen to break down the cellulose in grass into sugars that'll nourish me on my Alpine sojourn. While not ideal—as my artificial rumen won't be self-sustaining but instead reliant on injections of this enzyme—there are some advantages, too. Chief among these is I won't risk the possibility of giving myself some horrible parasitic infection. It'd basically just be like eating biological washing powder: could make you sick or kill you if you eat enough of it but won't actually start living inside you.

It's pretty expensive stuff, and, being an industrial product, it is sold in industrial quantities. But I eventually find the website of a supplier that will sell me less than 200 litres and for a reasonable price. It says they strictly supply only researchers affiliated with official establishments. Well, I'm arguably a researcher; my research question is somewhat unconventional and probably not quite the kind of thing the supplier means, but then who am I to judge what is and isn't research? And in any case, all you have to do is tick a box to say you're doing research and pick a name of a research institute from a drop-down list and job done—in the post.

*　*　*

I get on with preparations for my journey: contacting goatherds, trying to work out a route across the Alps, and casting my artificial rumen in silicone. It's a U-shaped bag, with a tube into which I will spit chewed-up grass and another tube from which I will suck the hopefully sugary enzymatically degraded product. It also includes a reservoir in the middle for the cellulase enzyme.

Things begin to move fast. Dr. Heath gets in touch to say they've pretty much finished my legs, and could I come up for a final fitting? I hop on the train. They're not quite what I was expecting, but I slip them on my arms. The front legs are solid; the back ankle-foot orthotics basically look like wedge heels, because basically that's what they are.

The look is cross-dresser at the back end, post–World War II NHS amputee patient at the front, but they work. I'm able to clomp around the workshop in fine quadruped fashion! Without the use of my hands, they're quite difficult to take off. So when Dr. Heath goes off to a meeting, I'm left to myself, sort of trapped as a goat. I start to get hungry, and there's a chocolate bar on the worktop, and the only way I can get into it is to grab the end of the wrapper between my teeth and shake violently, flinging the chocolate bar across the room. To get it back off the

Nice legs!

workshop floor I bend my wrists and lay my new forelegs flat on the floor, using my lips to nudge the chocolate bar into a position that I can attack with my teeth. Sure, it'd be easier if I just had a longer neck, but I'm managing, just about. When Dr. Heath returns and sees me struggling to eat the thing, quite unthinkingly he retrieves the half-chewed chocolate bar mostly still in its wrapper from the floor and feeds me the rest from his hand. I feel most goatlike.[1]

We complete the final modifications, and I thank Dr. Heath and Geoff, who wish me well with the trip.

"Don't bloody kill yourself," says Geoff.

* * *

The departure date is nearing, and I'm spending late nights making myself some less cross-dressy, more rugged, energy-returning rear-hoof prosthetics as well as a supportive kind of bodice. It also dawns on me that unless my mother wants me to freeze to death in the wind-driven rain of the Alps, she needs to help me make some sort of waterproof coat that'll fit over my goat parts. The first coat, being shiny pink polyester, does not help with the whole cross-dressing goat vibe, so I set her to work on something with more of a goatlike palette.

My bottle of cellulase enzyme arrives, and I stick it in the fridge per the storage instructions. There are a few warnings that it's *not* safe for human consumption, however. Are they just covering themselves, I wonder? I fire off an email to the supplier, mentioning a few aspects of what I'm intending to do and asking what sort of concentrations they'd recommend for digesting grass and so on.

I receive a short and stiffly worded email back, which begins: "Under no circumstances should you attempt what you suggest in your message below." It goes on to say that for a number of reasons (that they don't elucidate) what I propose may pose "significant health risks." The email also states that as I'm not associated with an institution with a defined and

---

1 Baaaaaaaaaaaaaaaa!

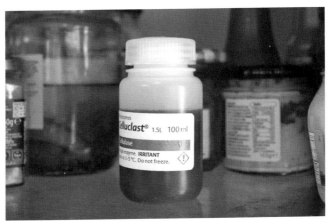

Irritant.

comprehensive health and safety policy, as I'd claimed, I should immediately "dispose of the enzyme by washing it down a drain with plenty of
water, or by flushing it down a toilet."

The next day I'm contacted by the Wellcome Trust. The supplier
of the enzyme has gotten in touch with them, too, and they're deeply
concerned. The "Trust would not support you undertaking this activity
against clear expert guidance." Furthermore, they note that in the corre-
spondence the supplier had forwarded to them, I had been talking about
"goats rather than elephants, as proposed in your application.…I would
be grateful if you would confirm receipt of this email and clarify the situation as a matter of urgency."

They want me to put all activity on hold and come in for a meeting.

Ahh, yes. The Wellcome Trust still thinks I'm doing a project about
elephants. I had forgotten to tell them about my early goat-related epiph-
any. Darn. With just days to go until the Alpine trip, this is bad news. I'm
not entirely sure why I didn't think to let the people who signed up to
fund an elephant project know that it had changed to a goat project, but
I genuinely think it's because Annette's words had just seemed so correct
to me. Or perhaps I was subconsciously following the advice of Werner
Herzog, that it's better to apologise than ask permission.

I prepare a presentation of justifications as to why goats are artistically, spiritually, and intellectually superior animals to try and become than elephants. It seems to go well, but the Trust remains unconvinced and asks me to keep things on hold while they discuss with the committee whether they can continue to be associated with this no-longer-elephant-related project.

Oh, dear. It couldn't have come at a more crucial time. To put everything on hold is just not possible. Weirdly enough, I've been contacted by a media company asking if I'm "interested in creating some YouTube content for a global drinks brand." Would attempting to become a goat in order to take a holiday from the existential pain of being a human fit with their brand values? If it means finishing the project, I guess I could brand myself. It'd be terribly painful though.

But the good old Wellcome Trust gets back in touch. And though they ask that I don't use the troublesome cellulase enzyme and that I *please* let them know if I'm thinking of making any more fundamental changes to the project, we're back on.

Without my cellulase, how am I going to digest grass? As a last resort, I purchase an Army-surplus pressure cooker that I hope is safe to use on a campfire. In my research into the methods the biofuel industry is developing to break down cellulose, I'd read about a process called "explosive steam treatment with acid hydrolysis." It involves heating plant material in a high-pressure chamber, then suddenly reducing the pressure, followed by heating with dilute acid. The process isn't practical for creating biofuels because the sugar yields aren't high enough and it requires an input of fuel to heat things up. It's not ideal for me, either, for the same reason, but I'm kind of desperate. My new plan is to chew up grass and spit it into my "rumen" to store it as I wander in the fields by day, then process the day's grass with the pressure cooker on a campfire at night using explosive steam treatment and acid hydrolysis, so I can eat and digest it. Not perfect, but I get Simon to take out his clothes so he can pack the pressure cooker in his bag, and off we go. The Swiss Alps beckon.

5

Goat Life

Bannalpsee, Wolfenschiessen, Switzerland
(sunny but cold)

Ahhhh, Switzerland. Home of immoral banking practices, half the world's largest particle accelerator, the relocated von Trapp family of *The Sound of Music*, and a goat farm high in the Alps that I've been communicating with via email.

My plan is to go and hang out as a goat with some of their goats, so I can learn their ways before attempting to cross the Alps to satisfy the conditions of my Wellcome Trust grant and thus hopefully mend some fences. I very much hope that spending time with the Alpine goats, going where they go, eating what they eat, and so on will effect an internal as well as an external change in my nature.

My niggling anxiety is that though I've arranged with the goat farmers to *stay* at their goat farm, I've not said what I'm hoping to do there, namely, the whole wearing of quadruped prosthetics and hanging out with their goats. The problem was that even trying to arrange the stay was difficult due to the language barrier. They claimed their English was terrible, but my *Schwiizertüütsch* is worse. Online translation helped with the to and fro of emails, but there were some odd-seeming outputs, which made me nervous about applying it to what would have to be a quite nuanced proposal, along the lines of "Could I come to your farm and eat grass and sleep with your goats?"

Switzerland: happiest nation on Earth according to the UN World Happiness Report.

At five o'clock in the morning, Simon, Tim—who'd come to take photos—and I had met at London Bridge. Now we have just caught the last cable car up the side of an Alp. The general inadequacy of my communications with the Alpine goat farm is rapidly becoming clear. Upon arriving at the upper cable car station, we see no sign of a goat farm. There is, however, a whole further stretch of mountain. The goat farm, according to Google Translate, is at the top of the Alp, and I assumed the cable car would pretty much take us the whole way there. Clearly not. So we'll just have to walk. Except the only way I can see to get to the top is a zigzagging path up an extremely steep-looking scree slope. Oh well, nothing for it. We're making our way across a dam that's holding back the waters of a beautiful mountain lake when we meet a man coming the other way. He looks oddly at us as I ask him in slow and loud English if this is the way to the farm at the top of the Alps.

Yes, he says, but you'll never get there with that. He's talking about my big suitcase on wheels, which is the smallest bag I'd been able to pack the goat legs and so on into. Simon and Tim have big rucksacks with equipment and food and clothes. He explains that there are two options for the route to the farm: either very long and more gentle, or shorter but up a path suitable "only for rock climbers." He's pretty emphatic that we'll

The Swiss man is adamant that a suitcase is not correct mountain-climbing equipment.

die if we try to do it with our luggage or at least that we'll be stuck on the side of the mountain overnight. We return with him to the little cable car station, where he gets in the cable car and…off it goes, the last cable car going down, leaving us to contemplate the peace and tranquility and failing light, halfway up an Alp.

Once again I find myself up a mountain, woefully underprepared, with my friend Simon.

"Right, there's nothing for it. We're going to have to bury our luggage and hike up the mountain before it gets dark." Simon begins to grumble. I'm looking around for a suitable place to start digging, when out of nowhere another Swiss man appears, this one very small and wearing a hat. I explain our predicament, and at first he doesn't appear to

Somewhere up there is our goat farm.

Loading up our luggage.

understand. I do some excellent gestural communication work, the penny drops, and he smiles gleefully and beckons us to follow him down a small hidden path away from the lake. At the end is another cable car; this one, however, is much more rickety. The "car" is an open wooden trough, its cables rising extremely steeply towards the top of the mountain. He smiles again, points at me and wags his finger, points at our luggage and nods his head, and off he dances, disappearing into the dark Alpine forest as suddenly as he'd appeared.

We load up the baggage trough and set off on foot. Presumably, the baggage car is operated from the top, where we need to get ourselves before it gets dark. The going, as promised, is steep, especially up the zig-zagging scree path, but after an hour or so we reach a plateau and head towards three buildings that must be the goat farm.

At last, the goat farm!

Maybe it's just the language barrier, maybe it's just their way, but the three goat farmers—Sepp, his wife, Rita, and their farmhand—seem reserved. In contrast, I'm in full hyped-up flow, saying a hundred words to every one of theirs but probably not getting across much more information. I'm nervous because at some point I'm going to need to let the cat out of the bag and introduce the purpose of our visit. The farm does offer overnight accommodation to walkers in the Alps, and, yes, I'm here to walk in the Alps, but I need to say that I intend to walk on four legs with their goats. The Swiss aren't known for embracing the unconventional. And admittedly I'm just further drawing on stereotype, but I don't think rural farmers are known for their love of experimental contemporary design practice, either.

I communicate to Sepp that we put our bags in the trough halfway down the mountain. Sepp acknowledges this with a nod and disappears into the farmhouse, leaving us to wander around. It's a beautiful spot: a grassy plateau between the craggy bulk of the remaining mountain rising up behind the farm and a vertiginous drop into the valley below. I can't see any goats, though.

We hear an engine sputter to life somewhere, and the big wheels of the baggage lift start hauling the cable and our trough of luggage up the mountain. As it comes to the top, Sepp appears, and as we unload our baggage, by way of conversation I ask where the goats are. He nods at the big shed.

"Cool," I say. "So you keep them inside for the night?"

He nods.

"So where shall we sleep?"

He nods at the big shed.

"Perfect," I say, and we follow Sepp into the barn. The accommodation is on a mezzanine above the goat floor (a kind of hayloft, I guess), and the barn echoes with the clanking of goat bells and is filled with the very strong smell of the herd below. Ideal. We get settled and start thinking about dinner. Tim and Simon have no intention of eating grass, and I, well, I'm not a goat yet. Sepp has started a fire in a little covered area next to the farmhouse, so we make our approach.

"Wow, a wood-fired bread oven! That's clever, Sepp! Mind if we join? And cook some things? Brill, thanks... So, nice weather? No? Raining all summer? Oh, that's a shame. It's getting pretty cold. Freezing? Yes, I suppose. That's why the goats are in the barn? Yes, thought so. I suppose you'll let them out again tomorrow to roam the Alps in the morning? No? Oh."

Sepp explains that it's getting too cold up here, the grass is getting patchy, and soon it'll snow, so tomorrow is going to be the day when he herds the goats from the high Alpine pastures in which they graze over the warm summer months, down the Alp to spend their winter in the valley. This migration has been the traditional way of grazing livestock in the Alps for perhaps five thousand years.

Right. I need to ask if Sepp will herd me, which for some reason is a slightly uncomfortable thing to ask a man you're barbecuing with.

"That goat migration sounds really interesting, Sepp. I don't suppose we could come along? If we like? Brilliant. And the thing is, Sepp, I'm doing this project. And, well, I was hoping I might sort of join the goats. Sort of with four legs? Sort of as one of your goats? If you see what I mean?"

Clanky, smelly roommates.

Our host, Sepp, fires the bread oven.

Now, I can see Sepp is not one for outbursts, so he just shifts his weight once he's asked a few questions to confirm what I'm communicating and sits, waiting for the bread oven to heat up, stroking his beard and considering.

"We start *early*," he says.

"That's fine. Great!" I say. "What time?"

"Four o'clock."

"OK, that's fine, great."

"We go...*quickly*," he says.

"Yep, that's OK. We'll just try and keep up!"

"We go down...*fast*." He angles his arm.

"Steep? Yes, it was steep on the way up. I'll just have to work that out myself and try and keep up, and if I can't, then obviously, that's my problem, Sepp, you won't have to worry about us at all."

"OK," says Sepp. He bids us good night and goes in to tell the farmhand that the oven is hot enough. That's that. We're on.

* * *

We're up before dawn. Even though it's still dark, the goats we're sharing the barn with are waking up, too. The clanking of their bells, which had died down over the freezing night, has picked up again. They're getting restless.

We can hear Sepp pottering around, too, so we go out to see what's happening. He tells us he's going to milk the goats, then we go. He disappears into our barn.

Sepp and Rita have a herd of about sixty peacock goats (no, the resemblance to peacocks isn't obvious to me, either). I wonder how long it's going to take for him to milk them all. We follow him in, and he's getting all the goats lined up with their heads sticking out through a gap in a special fence, tempted by their breakfast. The dim dawn light in the barn is suddenly transformed as a generator sparks to life, fluorescent lights flicker on, and, in a kind of surreal flourish, "Baby Love," the saccharine 1960s pop hit, starts blaring out of the speakers. The goats chow down, soothed by the sound of "Oooh-ah-oooh, baby love, my baby love"

Assembling my goat legs before dawn.

Man, machine, and goat.

et cetera. Sepp and the farmhand walk up the line, attaching their sucking milking machine to the udders of each goat in turn. Simon can't help but make jokes about Sepp attaching his milk suckers to my nipples. I'm *not* up for being milked. (And how would that even work, anyway? Actually, let's not pursue that question.) But yes, I had better start goating up, because Sepp and the farmhand and the goats know the milking drill, so it's not going to take long before they're finished.

I go and put on my goat suit: first my chest protector, then my "delayed-action artificial rumen," the waterproof suit my mother made me, my energy-returning back legs, my crash helmet, and, finally, my prosthetic front limbs.

This wasn't the entirety of my envisioned transformative suit. There were a few bits I'd just not managed to get working, most notably my goat eyes. I'd had a few detailed exchanges with an optical engineer about how to reposition my eyes to the side of my head and widen my field of vision to that of a goat, but bending light in the ways required is not a trivial matter. The solutions were either video goggles linked to wide-angle cameras, thus requiring batteries (which I wasn't keen on), or a system of glass prisms and lenses, which would have to be extremely large if they were to provide the 320-degree field of vision enjoyed by goats. A more compact prism system was available from a manufacturer of advanced periscopes for tanks; however, not being in the arms industry myself meant they were unwilling to engage with me, citing restrictive international law on sales of advanced military hardware. I was actually quite glad I'd not pursued goatlike eye adaptors, because I was starting to feel that I really didn't want to mess with my vision while walking around this perilous landscape on four legs.

Now, I'd obviously practised being a quadruped, with no end of walking round the prosthetics clinic and clomping round at home. But these had been flat and level stomping grounds, whereas the whole point of the Alps is that they're decidedly not level. I walk out of the elevated concrete pen in which I'd been getting changed and very quickly discover that walking downhill on four legs is extremely difficult. Even the slightest negative gradient is hard work. I stumble down the slope towards the

barn, straining and terrified of my front legs slipping from under me on
the wet stone. Rita, having observed this short demonstration of my goat
prowess, comes out of the farmhouse, visibly amused by this (let's be hon-
est) totally ridiculous spectacle of an Englishman finding it extremely difficult to be an Alpine goat.

"Very good—ha, ha, ha, ho, ho, ho. But they go fast, Thomas. You
shouldn't wait. You go now, and they'll catch you. They're very quick
down the rocky path, very excited, maybe dangerous for you if you're in
the way. You should get to the lake, where it's flat."

Right, then—a head start. I set off, but Jesus, it's hard going. Around
the farm is an undulating plateau. On level or even slightly upsloping
ground, I'm just about able to walk along with quite a lot of discomfort,
but there's no escaping that I'm heading in general *down* the mountain
to the lower winter pastures. And when I'm on even a slight downwards
slope, the strength required from my arms is draining. Dr. Heath and
Geoff have made my prosthetics so that about 60 percent of my weight
is taken through my front legs on level ground, but as the ground slopes
downwards, progressively more weight is borne through my front. And
lifting one front foot off the ground to take a step forwards means all that
weight needs to be taken by my other arm. Really what I'm doing is one-
arm press-ups down the side of a mountain. As I'm sure my girlfriend
would attest, I'm almost as strong as an ox, but I realise even that isn't
going to be strong enough unless the way down the mountain involves
quite a lot of going uphill.

Rita shouts out (though she doesn't have to shout too loud; when I
look back through my legs, I can see I've managed to walk a depressingly
short distance from the farm): "Thomas! You're too slow! Get down to
the lake! You need to be off the steep path before they come!"

The path Rita is referring to is the one we were warned off walking
up with our luggage yesterday: a steep zigzag of scree and loose boulders
with a stream/waterfall gushing down the middle of it.

Oh sweet Jesus. I'm already working up a sweat, and my knuckles,
despite being enveloped in Dr. Heath's special cushioning prosthetic silicone gel, are getting painful. I decide I need to follow Rita's advice and

get to the bottom of the narrow zigzag path before the goats come down it, as I really don't want to be in the way of a herd of excited goats. And so I invent a new sort of semibipedal—more tripedal—kind of gait. Using a mixture of sideways on four legs/frontways tottering on two while using a third leg against the slope for stability, sometimes going backwards, sometimes going forwards, I manage to scramble down the lethal path. Just as I'm nearly to the lake at the bottom, Rita's voice echoes around the valley as she shouts from the top, "They're coming!"

I turn and look back up the slope, and there's Sepp and the farmhand at the front of a column of excited goats. When they've crossed the bottleneck of the bridge at the top, there's nothing to hold them back, and they seem to almost flow like the stream down the mountainside. I don't wait. I get to the bottom of the slope and set off along the lakeside as fast as my four legs can carry me. Which isn't all that fast. I've not gotten far before the first of the herd I aspire to join makes a break to get past me, then slows to a trot. Another passes at a fast trot, followed by another, and another, then the farmhand, who strides by waving a stick and loudly encouraging us goats with "*Chumm jetze! Chumm jetze!*"

The reaction of the other goats to me isn't all that encouraging. I can see they're bunched up behind me as I clank and huff and puff along, until they get the nerve to get past me. The frequency of goats going past increases. I'm still blundering along, desperately trying to keep up, but when I try to break into a trot myself, I stumble and only just manage to stop myself going face-first into the gravel. This is an even worse prospect given that my deeply ingrained instinct to stop my face from scraping along the ground has been compromised by having two front legs Velcroed to my forearms.

The main body of the herd swarms past, followed by a few stragglers, then finally by Sepp bringing up the rear.

"Too slowwww," he drawls as he strides past. Sweat is dripping off the end of my nose. My arms are on fire, and I can't really feel my knuckles, but I imagine there's not all that much skin left on them. All I can do is watch as the last few goats trot along the path at the end of the lakeside, over the bank of the earth dam, and are gone.

I struggle on a few more metres, but I know it's in vain. The bleats of the herd are fading out of earshot, and then I'm the only goat, a lonely goat, high on a hill. All the misgivings of Professor Hutchinson and Dr. Heath and Geoff come painfully to mind. I've managed to keep up with the real goats for maybe 750 metres…Let's say a kilometre. Not very good, I know, but until you've had to do one-arm push-ups for a kilometre with some excited goats moving at a fast trot, then, gentle reader, I don't think you're in a position to criticise. If I sound defensive, well, I think it's because I'm so disappointed. For a moment I'd felt the exhilaration of moving as part of the herd, but all too soon the moment has passed.

With no goats around to see me, I do a very ungoatlike thing. I take a seat on a rock and contemplate the situation.

It's pretty clear there's nothing for it. I'm just going to have to take it slow and make my own way down the mountain to the winter pasture.

I feel a bit more relaxed travelling at a walk and not trying to keep up with the trotting goats, and the going is slow but steady. I follow the track beside the lake for another couple of kilometres, then cross the long earth-bank dam, and start heading down the path to the valley below.

My short neck comes back to haunt me.

*   *   *

It's some hours before I arrive down in the valley and sight what I hope is my herd of goats, grazing contentedly in fields surrounding a lone farmhouse. I don't want to be shot by a Swiss farmer mistaking me for some strange goat-man-beast intent on worrying his animals, so I figure it best to ask politely at the farmhouse. The farmer, Tomas, answers the door, but Sepp is there, too, extremely surprised to see us. I say I'd like to rejoin the herd. Sepp defers to Tomas: "They're his goats down here."

"Be my guest," says Tomas.

After negotiating several electric fences, I'm able to rejoin the herd on the slopes of their new pasture, which is covered in every goat's desire, fresh green grass. And so, gentle reader, finally I am living the goat life.

Ahhhh, the goat life. This consists of walking to a patch of grass and eating it for five minutes or so. Walking to another patch of grass, eating that. And so on and so forth. I begin to learn the subtleties of the different types of grass: the blue-green patches of grass are bitter, whereas the greener-green grass is sweet and much preferable.

Chew, chew, chew. Spit chewed grass into tube from the prosthetic rumen bag strapped to my torso. Walk to new patch of grass. As foreseen, there is the slight difficulty of actually getting my mouth to the grass because of my inconveniently short neck. The system I develop is basically getting down on my forelegs and planting my face in a particularly green patch, tearing off as much grass as I can fit in my mouth, then getting back to my feet and chewing it over before spitting it into my rumen for later.

I also discover I'm really quite good at being a goat as long as I'm moving uphill. Yes, I'm a most curious animal: a goat that can only go up. And now that I'm not clanking and huffing and puffing along, but just calmly walking around eating grass as a goat should, my fellow goats are much more accepting. Curious even. I wonder what they think of me. A couple come over to check me out, sniffing at my face. I try and sniff back, ignoring my human physical aversion to the powerful smell of their breath: a deep odour of fermenting grass, like distilled farmer's silage. Though a few seem a bit scared at first, once they see me enjoying the grass like them, they stop avoiding me. And one goat in particular, goat number eighteen, is a goat I seem to spend most of my day wandering around with. It's kind of nice: I wander after her when she moves to another patch of grass, and likewise when I move off, she's not far behind.

However, my propensity for only going uphill means that eventually I find I've wandered into the middle of things and become nearly the highest goat on the hillside. I happen to look up from grazing, and I realise that the entire herd is looking at me. It's suddenly gotten very quiet. Everyone's stopped chewing.

It's like the part in a Western when the entire saloon suddenly falls silent because the newcomer has done something provocative, something that threatens to upset the established scheme. And I'm looking, and all the other goats are looking back, and I'm starting to feel a little bit uneasy because those horns are actually quite pointy, and some of these goats are about as big as I am, and I become very much aware that they're far stronger and more agile, too.

It had all been going so well, but I may have inadvertently committed a goat faux pas. I remember reading that being the highest up in a

herd can be a display of dominance. I think I may have just challenged the dominance hierarchy without realising it. Oops.

I'm kind of ashamed to say that I'm thinking that if it's going to come to a fight, I can probably give a pretty good right hook with my prosthetic front leg. I say "ashamed" because a goat doesn't box; I should be thinking of butting with my head. In a choice between fighting like a goat and so being put in my place at the bottom of the pecking order or fighting dirty and establishing myself somewhere higher up, I am poised for the latter.

In any case, it doesn't come to that. I think it's goat number eighteen who steps in and diffuses the situation. She breaks the impasse by simply walking through the middle of the group and starting to wander. The other goats take their cue from her, and the palpable tension in the herd drains away. We get back to wandering and eating, and all drift over the brow of the hill.

* * *

And that's how I could spend the next week…Except, of course, towards
the end of the day it starts raining, and though my mother's waterproof suit
holds up for a while, the sweat that I've generated with my exertions means
I'm pretty damp anyway, and it's not too long before I start shivering. And
despite all the grass I start getting rather hungry. And my feet are cold. And
the prospect of spending the night out here in the field as the temperature
drops near or below freezing really starts to seem not very fun. And I start
to think of how nice it would be to have a nice, warm fire.

* * *

I've eaten more grass in one day than I've eaten in my whole life up to
this point. Even though I've been spitting it into my artificial rumen bag,
the process of chewing it up has inevitably involved swallowing some of
it. I quite like the taste of grass, but, of course, lacking the amazing internal bacteria farm of a goat's rumen, I've managed to derive very little in
the way of nutrition from the grass I've eaten. It's time to get the pressure
cooker out.

We find a spot, and I build a human campfire, with my human
hands. Everything I've read says to not put a pressure cooker on a campfire due to the risk of uneven heating and explosion and so on, but by this
stage I'm beyond caring. I empty my rumen bag of chewed up grass into
the pot, screw down the lid, stick it on the fire, and stand back.

It doesn't take too long before the little weight on the pressure
cooker's valve starts being bumped up by steam, indicating the pressure inside the vessel has built up. I lift it off the campfire. The explosive
part of the protocol for explosive steam treatment refers to the sudden
change of pressure needed to break down the fibrous structures the molecules of cellulose make up, so acid can then break them down into sugars.
I hope in this instance it isn't actually going to mean explosive, as I gin-
gerly unscrew the knob clamping on the lid. Steam whistles out as I release
the pressure. Inside is a kind of grass soupy stew, slightly burnt at the bottom. It doesn't look very appetising at all. I add some acetic acid (vinegar)

The muddy orange colour indicates the presence of sugars.

Delicious!

to the (hopefully) partially broken down fibrous grass and put the pressure cooker back on the fire for the acid to hydrolyse the cellulose into some lovely, energy-giving sugars. After a few minutes more I decide it's time to eat. But what exactly will I be eating? Indigestible fibre, or delicious sugar?

I've brought a chemical called Benedict's reagent with me, which can be used as a simple test for the presence of sugars in a solution. Basically, you add a few drops to a sample of what you want to test, boil it up, and if it turns orange, there's sugar present. Time for some campfire chemistry.

I put a bit of my grass-stewy soup into a test tube, add the Benedict's solution, and heat it up in a water bath on the remains of the campfire. It's gotten dark, but by torchlight I can see: the sample has turned orange! Well, technically a muddy brown, but it is definitely more orange than it was before. There's at least some sort of sugar in there! And sugar means energy!

I tuck into the most unappetising meal of my life: burnt grass stew. It doesn't taste particularly sweet. Nor does it seem to me particularly nutritious. I consider the potential for the Goat Diet and decide it tastes bad enough to be a goer with a bit of marketing.

* * *

When we finally get back to the farm, Rita invites us for dinner at the farmhouse. Never have I been so grateful. It's so nice and cosy inside. Rita has cooked a big pot of goat stew, which we eat with bread and goat cheese. I indulge in cannibalism. It's disturbing, but, after a day eating nothing but grass, quite delicious. Disturbing. But delicious. But oh, so disturbing. But really, really delicious.

Sepp and Rita are understandably curious as to the purpose of the day's events. I explain all about it and that it began with the idea of escaping human worries.

"You're from the city," says Sepp. "That's why you're crazy. Up here you wouldn't need such a crazy idea."

They've not been down the mountain to the town for months, though Rita will have to go soon to sell some of the goat cheese she makes. She's not looking forward to it. I can see Sepp's point. If becoming a goat is about leading a simple life, well, *perhaps* a simpler way would be to become a goat farmer rather than a goat.

"Where do you go after here?"

"Well, I need to try and cross the Alps."

"Ha! You should be an ibex."

I ask if he's ever seen an ibex. He has, many times. They're amazing creatures, able to survive up here even during the snowbound winters. He tells us that sometimes an ibex will come down from the mountain and get in with the goats and breed, but the baby—

"You can't handle them. They just jump over all the fences."

Sepp tells me something encouraging. He'd spoken to Tomas, the goat farmer from the valley, who'd been observing my exploits in his fields: "Tomas says you were accepted by the herd."

"Really?…I mean, I thought I was."

"Yes, he said he saw you, and you were accepted by them."

And so perhaps for a while the goats thought of me as a goat and I thought of myself as a goat, and so maybe for a moment…

* * *

Sepp buckles a goat bell around my neck. I'm part of his herd now.

We stay at the farm for three days. I'm able to learn a lot about how my legs work in rough terrain and how goats manage to move so well despite not looking at their feet, and I get slightly better at going downhill, but all too soon it's time to become more ibexlike and set off to cross the Alps. As we're preparing to leave, Sepp buckles one of his goat bells around my neck. I feel accepted by goat herd and goatherd, but I have to leave: I have a promise to fulfil. A promise made by a man, to be kept as a goat. We walk away, into the mountains, and…forgive me, gentle reader, but very soon we come to a bridge, and I trip-trap, trip-trap across the bridge from the real world into fantasy. Our way is hard, involving many trials and tribulations. I eat much delicious grass.

We go up and up and up, and finally we reach a glacier. At the top of the glacier is where Switzerland ends and Italy begins. Climbing the glacier means we will have crossed the Alps, with just the slope down into Italy remaining.

A man falls from the sky and asks me what I'm doing. I say, "Some men dream of being a bird. I dream of being a goat."

"Yah, cool!" he says. I continue climbing and climbing. Do we make it? Near enough.

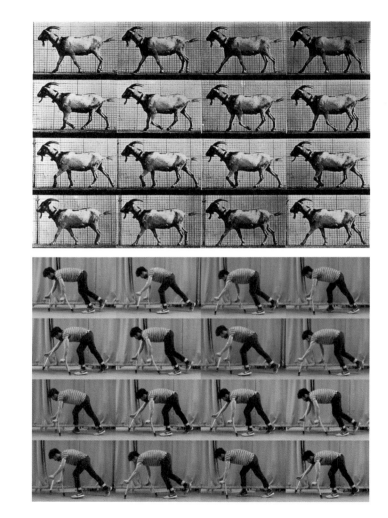

ACKNOWLEDGMENTS

I know it is but a modest volume, so pages of thank-yous may seem a bit overblown. However, they're entirely warranted because many people helped me with this project to become a goat, even though it is (I now realise, probably) impossible (at least in my framing of reality). And a whole further load of people helped with making it into this second book (which I found far more difficult and which took much longer than I expected), which is soon to be sent out in to the world (an exciting but rather nerve-wracking prospect. Crikey). I'm a designer, crossing sideways across academic disciplines in pursuit of something that...well, I hope it's at least sort of original, and I know I've not been able to do justice to the depth of detail, the dirt of the arguments, the towers of evidence built up over decades, which mean "we" can say we know something about ourselves and other animals. And every time I wrote "we know" it was because someone has actually gone somewhere with a trowel or a note-pad, or tried something out, and usually not found anything. But occasionally, someone has found something, and they and others have had the benefit of an education such that they have recognised it as something, and have been able to write about it, and it has become part of one of these towers of evidence that have made my attempt to become a goat interesting for me to do (and, I really hope, interesting for you to read about, gentle reader).

My thanks and gratitude to: Sioban Imms for her help, support, and love. Simon Gretton, friend, videographer, editor extraordinaire, for being part of another harebrained scheme, and watching me a lot, again. The Wellcome Trust for funding my attempt to become an elephant (and sticking with it when I'd metamorphosed), without which neither the project nor this book would've happened. Tim Bowditch for not only his brilliant photography, but a whole load of other stuff besides. Daniel Alexander for his brilliant photography despite the tuberculosis risk. Sara Stemen for editing this book and putting up with my many vacillations, Paul Wagner for designing it, and all at Princeton Architectural Press for publishing it.

The Thwaites family. The Imms family. The Percy-Xu family. Kitty Nunnely for her reassurance and insightful comments on drafts of this book, Noggin Nunnely, and the rest of the Nunnely family. The Wayman family (especially Vito for managing to write to the Queen [who still hasn't written back]). Steve Furlonger at Windsor Workshop Ltd. for all his help and support with this project (legs *and* rumen), as well as with my other attempts at making stuff in his workshop over the last twenty years.

Austin Houldsworth for photographing me making a twat of myself (and welcome to the crazy world, *Thomas* Houldsworth!). Vera Marin for invaluable assistance. YiWen Tseng for help with bones, both physical and digital. Liam McGarry, who I hope is enjoying New Zealand. Harry Trimble for his writing and math skills. Bernd Hopfengärtner for his drone piloting and German skills. Michael and Kerran for letting me have my Goat Show at their Studio 1.1 Gallery. Akademie Schloss Solitude for the time to develop this project, and the workshop space to make Prototype Number 2. Allan Newton for explaining the limitations of prisms and optical fibre bundles.

Soul—Annette Høst for her genuine, wise, and frank advice.

Mind—Bob, Gower, and all at Buttercups Sanctuary for Goats for the work they do and for helping me so much with mine. Dr. Alan McElligott, Luigi Baciadonna, and Dr. Juliane Kaminski for goat chats. Dr. Joe Devlin for indulging my brain's wish to be zapped.

Body—Dr. Glyn Heath and Geoff for their prosthetics work, fun, and insight. Professor John Hutchinson for being so generous with his time and knowledge. Dr. Alexander Stoll for dissecting with me, Sophie Regnault for dissecting with me twice, and Richard Prior for cleaning Venus's bones. Ivan Thorley of Puppets with Guts for metal work, tea, and sympathy.

Guts—Dr. Alison Kingston-Smith and Professor Jamie Newbold at Aberystwyth University for telling me all about their rumen work.

Goat Life—Rita and Joseph Waser.

206

Selected Bibliography

FOREWORD

Becker, Ernest. *The Denial of Death*. New York: Free Press, 1985.

SOUL

Aubert, Maxime, Adam Brumm, M. Ramli, Thomas Sutikna, E. Wahyu Saptomo, B. Hakim, M. J. Morwood, Gerrit D. van den Bergh, Leslie Kinsley, and Anthony Dosseto. "Pleistocene cave art from Sulawesi, Indonesia." *Nature* 514, no. 7521 (2014): 223–27.

Bednarik, Robert G. "Pleistocene palaeoart of Africa." *Arts* (Multidisciplinary Digital Publishing Institute) 2, no. 1 (2013): 6–34.

McComb, Karen, Lucy Baker, and Cynthia Moss. "African elephants show high levels of interest in the skulls and ivory of their own species." *Biology letters* 2, no. 1 (2006): 26–28.

Willerslev, Rane. *Soul Hunters: Hunting, Animism, and Personhood Among the Siberian Yukaghirs*. Oakland: University of California Press, 2007.

MIND

Briefer, Elodie F., and Alan G. McElligott. "Rescued goats at a sanctuary display positive mood after former neglect." *Applied Animal Behaviour Science* 146, no. 1 (2013): 45–55.

Briefer, Elodie F., Federico Tettamanti, and Alan G. McElligott. "Emotions in goats: mapping physiological, behavioural and vocal profiles." *Animal Behaviour* 99 (2015): 131–43.

Clayton, Nicola S., and Anthony Dickinson. "Mental Time Travel: Can Animals Recall the Past and Plan for the Future?" *Encyclopedia of Animal Behavior* (2010): 438–42.

McBrearty, Sally, and Alison S. Brooks. "The revolution that wasn't: a new interpretation of the origin of modern human behavior." *Journal of human evolution* 39, no. 5 (2000): 453–63.

Pinker, Steven. *The Better Angels of Our Nature*. New York: Viking, 2011.

Slobodchikoff, C. N., William R. Briggs, Patricia A. Dennis, and Anne-Marie C. Hodge. "Size and shape information serve as labels in the alarm calls of Gunnison's prairie dogs Cynomys gunnisoni." *Current Zoology* 58, no. 5 (2012): 741–48.

Sommer, Volker, and Amy R. Parish. "Living Differences: The Paradigm of Animal Cultures." In *Homo Novus–A Human Without Illusions*. Edited by Ulrich J. Frey, Charlotte Störmer, and Kai Willführ, 19–33. Heidelberg: Springer, 2010.

Suddendorf, Thomas. *The Gap: The Science of What Separates Us from Other Animals*. New York: Basic Books, 2013.

Wrangham, Richard. "Did Homo sapiens self-domesticate?" (presented at the CARTA symposium "Domestication and Human Evolution," Salk Institute for Biological Studies, California, October 10, 2014. carta.anthropogeny. org/events/domestication-and-human-evolution.

BODY

Wilson, Frank R. *The Hand*. New York: Pantheon Books, 1998.

GUTS

Chandel, Anuj K., et al. "Dilute Acid Hydrolysis of Agro-Residues for the Depolymerization of Hemicellulose: State-of-the-Art." In *D-Xylitol: Fermentative Production, Application and Commercialization*." Edited by Silvio Silvério da Silva and Anuj Kumar Chandel. New York: Springer Life Sciences, 2012.

Kingston-Smith, Alison H., Joan E. Edwards, Sharon A. Huws, Eun J. Kim, and Michael Abberton. "Plant-based strategies towards minimising 'livestock's long shadow.'" *Proceedings of the Nutrition Society* 69, no. 4 (2010): 613–20.

Sun, Ye, and Jiayang Cheng. "Hydrolysis of lignocellulosic materials for ethanol production: a review." *Bioresource Technology* 83, no. 1 (2002): 1–11.

Van Nood, Els, Anne Vrieze, Max Nieuwdorp, Susana Fuentes, Erwin G. Zoetendal, Willem M. de Vos, and Caroline E. Visser, et al. "Duodenal infusion of donor feces for recurrent Clostridium difficile." *New England Journal of Medicine* 368, no. 5 (2013): 407–15.

GOAT LIFE

"De tre bukkene Bruse." In *Norske Folkeeventyr*. Edited by Peter Christen Asbjørnsen and Jørgen Moe (1843).

Credits

Front of jacket, 2–4: Tim Bowditch

INTRODUCTION

14 left: © Brooks Kraft/Corbis
14 right: Mark Nunnely
16: Jenny Paton, Wellcome Trust

CHAPTER 1: SOUL

18–19: Richard Erdoes, San Juan Pueblo deer dance, ca. 1977. Courtesy of Beinecke Rare Book and Manuscript Library, Yale University
23 top: Thomas Thwaites

23 bottom: Benjamin Waterhouse Hawkins, *Man, and the elephant*. From Benjamin Waterhouse Hawkins, *A comparative view of the human and animal frame* (1860), plate six. Courtesy of University of Wisconsin Digital Collections Center

24 top left: Frank Stuart, Nellie, circa 1950. Courtesy of Reuben Hoggett, cyberneticzoo.com

24 top right: "Cybernetic Anthropomorphous Machine" constructed by General Electric in the 1960s. Courtesy of miSci, Museum of Innovation & Science, Schenectady, New York.

24 bottom: Guilhem Vellut, *Les Machines de l'Ile at Nantes*, 2012. flickr.com/photos/o_0/7936101566. Creative Commons BY 2.0. Cropped from original.

29, 30: Thomas Thwaites

32 top: Nicolaas Witsen, *een Schaman ofte Duyvel-priester*. From *Noord en Oost Tartaryen: Behelzende eene beschryving van verschiedene Tartersche en nabuurige gewesten* (M. Schalekamp, 1705), 662. Ghent University, digitised by Google Books

32 middle: Alphonso Roybal, *Hunters' or Deer Dance*, ca. 1932. From C. Szwedzicki, *Pueblo Indian painting; 50 reproductions of watercolor paintings* (Nice, France, 1932). Courtesy of the University of Cincinnati Libraries, Archives and Rare Books Library

32 bottom, left and right: Richard Erdoes, San Juan Pueblo Deer Dance, ca. 1977. Courtesy of Beinecke Rare Book and Manuscript Library, Yale University

35: *Löwenmensch* of Hohlenstein-Stadel. Photograph: © Sabrina Stoppe. Courtesy of Ulmer Museum, Ulm, Germany

36 top: Pendant du Sorcier, Salle du Fond at Chauvet-Pont-d'Arc Cave (Ardèche, France). Photograph: J.-M. Geneste © MCC/Centre National de Préhistoire

36 bottom: The Shaft Scene at Lascaux Cave (Dordogne, France). Photograph: N. Aujoulat © MCC/Centre National de Préhistoire

37 top: Breuil H, *Un dessin de la grotte des Trois frères at Grotte des Trois-Frères* (Ariège, France), 1930. From *omptes rendus des séances de l'Académie des Inscriptions et Belles-Lettres*, 74e année, N. 3, 1930, 261–64. Courtesy of Wellcome Library, London. Creative Commons BY 4.0

37 bottom: Breuil H, *Homme masque en Bison at Grotte des Trois-Frères* (Ariège, France), ca. 1930. From ibid. Courtesy of Wellcome Library, London. Creative Commons BY 4.0

CHAPTER 2: MIND
48–49: Sioban Imms
51: Vera Marin
52, 53: Thomas Thwaites
62: © Araldo de Luca/Corbis
64: Baby being fed milk directly from a goat's teat, Postcard, Havana, Cuba (Havana: C. Jordi, ca. 1930). Courtesy of Wellcome Library, London. Creative Commons BY 4.0
70: Liberia Official Scott O48 5c Stamp, Chimpanzee, 1906. bigblue1840-1940.blogspot.co.uk/2013/07/ClassicStampsofLiberia1860-1914.html
77, 81, 82: Sioban Imms

CHAPTER 3: BODY
86–87: Tim Bowditch
89: Vera Marin
91: Tim Bowditch
93: Tim Bowditch
95–102: Thomas Thwaites
103: © Fahad Shadeed/Reuters/Corbis
104, 107: Thomas Thwaites
110, 112: Austin Houldsworth
114, 115: Thomas Thwaites
117, 118, 119 left: Daniel Alexander
119 right: Gerard de Lairesse, Engraving of a dissected human arm, 1685. Plate from *Anatomia Humani Corporis* (Bidloo, 1685). Courtesy of Wellcome Library, London. Creative Commons BY 4.0
120, 121: Liam Finn McGarry

CHAPTER 4: GUTS
122–23: Thomas Thwaites
125: Daniel Alexander
126, 128: Thomas Thwaites
129: YiWen Tseng
130: Thomas Thwaites
136: Dr. Glynn Heath
138: Thomas Thwaites

CHAPTER 5: GOAT LIFE
140–201: Tim Bowditch
202 top: Eadweard Muybridge, *A goat walking*, 1887. (Philadelphia: University of Pennsylvania, 1887). Courtesy of Wellcome Library, London. Creative Commons BY 4.0
203 bottom: Austin Houldsworth
205: Tim Bowditch

Supported by
wellcometrust

PUBLISHED BY
Princeton Architectural Press
A McEvoy Group company
37 East Seventh Street
New York, New York 10003
www.papress.com

EDITOR: Sara Stemen
DESIGNER: Paul Wagner

SPECIAL THANKS TO: Nicola Bednarek Brower, Janet Behning, Erin Cain,
Tom Cho, Barbara Darko, Benjamin English, Jenny Florence, Jan Cigliano Hartman,
Lia Hunt, Mia Johnson, Valerie Kamen, Simone Kaplan-Senchak, Stephanie Leke,
Diane Levinson, Jennifer Lippert, Sara McKay, Jaime Nelson, Rob Shaeffer,
Joseph Weston, and Janet Wong of Princeton Architectural Press
—Kevin C. Lippert, publisher

LIBRARY OF CONGRESS CATALOGING-IN-PUBLICATION DATA
Thwaites, Thomas, 1980– author.
GoatMan : how I took a holiday from being human /
Thomas Thwaites. — First edition.
        pages   cm
Includes bibliographical references.
ISBN 978-1-61689-405-4 (alk. paper)
1. Thwaites, Thomas, 1980—Themes, motives. 2. Psychology—
Miscellanea. 3. Goats—Miscellanea. I. Title.
NK1447.6.T49A35 2016
745.4092—dc23
                        2015028271